The Footballer's Journey

Real-World Advice on Becoming and Remaining a Professional Footballer

Dean Caslake
Guy Branston

Published by Bennion Kearny Limited
6 Woodside, Churnet View Road
Oakamoor. ST10 3AE

www.BennionKearny.com

Cover image:

www.daniellevictoriaprints.co.uk

Acknowledgements

A massive thank you must go out to all the professional footballers (both current and former) that took time out of their busy schedules (with no financial reward) to provide the valuable and inspiring contributions that have really brought this book to life!

Their contributions have helped shed light on what is required to make a living in the game as well as providing incredible advice and guidance that can really help readers shape their own footballing journeys.

We would also like to thank James, and everyone at Bennion Kearny, for their support, dedication, and hard work throughout the process of creating *The Footballer's Journey*.

Foreword

The Footballer's Journey is essential reading. It helps guide and advise not only football hopefuls, but also parents, and even current professionals when looking at life after football.

As stated in the book, you often need luck, but it's also vital for you to be disciplined. When I was younger, both my brothers were great players and were both at Millwall. Through ill-discipline at 16 they both got kicked out. Consequently, when I was 16, the club moved me to the other side of London where I stayed in digs, keeping me out of trouble and stopping me from going out on Friday nights.

At 16 you are meeting your mates and they are talking about great nights they've had, and how many girls they've met, and you miss out on all that. But it's all worth it. When you achieve your dream it's fantastic.

The most important thing to realize is that football does stop and doesn't last forever. When I played, if you weren't a top player playing for a top club, you would have to find other work, and earn money after football to pay your mortgage. I was lucky in that respect; I played for some top teams and I got my pension at 35. You've got to be switched on to put money into a pension, you need to put money away for a rainy day.

Looking at life after football, when players do finish in the game, the stats say that three-out-of-five are divorced within the first four years of retirement. It happened to me. You've been so disciplined all the way through your career, but I then reached 35 and turned into an 18 year old again. I started to party, ended up divorced, and in rehab. Take note of this book's advice regarding life after football! Not only in terms of career choices but also lifestyle choices.

There are some other figures that support the massive importance of preparing for life after football. Did you know, for example, that there are over 200 ex pros in prison? The reality of the football world is that once a club no longer requires your services - you are gone; they are not going to look out for you. Be sure to look out for yourself.

This book also talks about education. Education is really important and you should explore other avenues outside football. The worst thing is for a kid at 16, who has been playing football for years, to be let go with nothing to fall back on. Not preparing for the future is naïve given the small number of schoolboy footballers who progress into the professional game.

The problem with young lads is clear. Everyone thinks they are going to make it, so they don't bother with a backup plan. Hopefully, a book like this will provide the advice and real life examples to make kids think about arranging something to fall back on.

Meaningful advice is great, and there is plenty within this book. When we are young we think we know it all. We all think we are going to be footballers. We all think we are not going to get injured, everyone is going to love us, and we won't have bad games. This book certainly gives lots of good advice into the realities of the industry. If the advice is taken in a positive manner - rather than being seen as criticism - it can be a very useful tool for football hopefuls, parents, and young pros.

To finish I would like to offer some advice to all football hopefuls. I think it's very important to listen to advice, but the main thing is to play your hardest every time you put that football kit on. It doesn't matter if it's training, if you are running up and down hills, or if you are in the gym. Always play your hardest. Always give your all. Your ambition in football should be to play your hardest in every single game and that will get you further than anything else.

Enjoy the book, take note, and I wish you good luck with your own footballing journey.

All the Best

Neil 'Razor' Ruddock

(Former England, QPR, Millwall, Tottenham Hotspur, Southampton, Liverpool, West Ham, Crystal Palace & Swindon)

About the Authors

Dean Caslake is a graduate from Bournemouth University where he gained a BA studying Finance and Business. At Bournemouth, Dean was a member of the university's most successful football team that reached the national cup final and achieved a second place finish in the BUCS Premier South division.

Dean has always had a keen interest in football and, growing up, Dean was considered by some to have a degree of talent in the game. Ultimately, like many young hopefuls across the country, he failed to impress and make the step up into the professional game. He has forever remained an amateur player.

Since failing to progress to a professional level, Dean has always been left wondering what other players 'had' that he didn't? He wanted to know what the professionals - the people you see on a Saturday afternoon - had done differently to put themselves in the position they are in. Dean wanted to explore these unanswered questions further and "The Footballer's Journey" was born.

Guy Branston is a professional footballer currently plying his trade at Plymouth Argyle. Guy has been involved in professional football for nearly 20 years. After playing for 19 professional clubs and making 26 moves within his career, Guy has had more setbacks than most; this gives him ' Premier League' insight into what qualities are needed to succeed in this up and down game.

Guy also runs the website allaboutballerz.com alongside his professional football commitments. The website allaboutballerz.com provides a platform for footballers at any level to put themselves out there and get noticed. Guy works with players on a daily basis in order to help them stay in the game. This is the main reason why he wanted to be involved with The Footballer's Journey - a book that looks into the real world of professional football.

Table of Contents

1

Stepping onto the Footballing Ladder

As with career development for most professions – your first step on the footballing ladder requires you to get yourself noticed and put yourself 'out there'. Subsequently, you look to give yourself the best possible chance of moving up the ladder and progressing in your chosen field. There may be an element of luck involved, possibly chance, and possibly being in the right place at the right time, but these things can only take you so far. Ultimately you make your own luck!

The main difference between football and other industries is that you have to grow up fast; the footballing journey can begin as early as seven or eight years old.

Don't know what's expected of you

On trial days (or even in some matches) if the manager hasn't clearly outlined your role in the team, it's hard to know exactly what's expected of you or judge what qualities a certain scout and/or manager wants to see. But one thing you have to realize is that everyone is different and opinions change from scout to scout, manager to manager.

An important aspect to getting yourself noticed is ensuring you bring something a bit different to the table - to help catch the eye; this must come not only from natural footballing ability but personal qualities such as commitment, temperament and organisation. It's likely that scouts and managers will also look at your awareness on the pitch and focus on your reading of the game and positional sense.

Traditionally, scouts have been fascinated with players' physical attributes (such as height and strength) as determinants of whether or not they can progress in the game. However, in recent times, as football has developed, scouting systems have had to change. Teams such as Barcelona, who have a number of fantastically gifted football players, who barely stand over five feet tall, have helped change the longstanding mindsets of scouts and managers. Many have now moved away from the belief that you must meet a certain height, or certain build, to become a top professional.

This should be your inspiration for continuing to strive towards achieving your goal even if physical attributes have been identified as an issue during a trial period. If you have footballing ability, and have the burning desire to become a professional footballer, don't let anyone convince you you're not going to make it because you're too small or not strong enough. The way football is evolving - this simply isn't the case.

"Football is filled with setbacks and the biggest setbacks I had, were at the age of 14/15, because I went from being one of the top players to just being told by Kilmarnock that I wasn't quite there physically, and I was a wee bit slow. That was probably the biggest thing because, at that time, other players are going off to play full time and you're wondering what you're going to do.

That's when I made the step to go and play in Glasgow, away from Ayrshire. Ayrshire has its own football community, so to go and play in Glasgow for Queens Park was a big step.

Comments could set me back, and they were all to do with my physicality, I remember one quote a scout made - "If he was quick he'd be going to Manchester United." At the time I thought that was fair enough as, at the end of the day, they had to make a decision. But my Dad, for example, was 6'4" so they knew I was going to grow. I wasn't heavy or anything. I was slim and always had the agility to be mobile."

Neill Collins - Sheffield United FC

> *"I was rejected by Manchester United for being "too fat" which wasn't nice to hear. Also, later in my career, I trialled at Hearts who told me I was too small (5'9" and 12 stone)."*
>
> **Kevin Nicholson - Torquay United FC**

Footballing potential can be recognised at any time

Players can be scouted for a professional club at any time and at any age. Whether you're an eight year-old playing for your school team, or an 18 year-old young man playing non-league football for your local club, there is always a chance to achieve your dream, so don't give up. You don't always have to go through a professional club's academy system to make your dream a reality.

> *"I went to trial with Sunderland when I finished my contract after two years with Dumbarton. Mick McCarthy was the manager at the time and after a two-week trial he signed me. I came straight out of university and signed for Sunderland. It isn't really something that happens too often."*
>
> **Neill Collins - Sheffield United FC**

> *"I was scouted from Ryman League, Division One South club, Faversham Town FC at the age of 18. They are at stage eight of the football league pyramid. I was never part of an academy when I was growing up."*
>
> **Jack Baldwin - Peterborough United FC**

> *"At the age of 11, I was scouted by Crystal Palace at my district trials. After a trial they offered me a contract until I was 14, they then offered me another two years to take me up to the age of 16. The age of 16 was when they offered me a two year scholarship."*
>
> **Matt Fish - Gillingham FC**

> *"I was scouted first of all by Nottingham Forest at eight years old. However, at nine years old Leicester approached me as well and, because I lived in Leicester, I went to Leicester City instead."*
>
> **Matt Piper - Former Leicester City FC & Sunderland AFC**

> *"I got to about 15 (around the time when you are thinking about leaving school), looking to get an apprenticeship and I was lucky really. My local team, Bolton, was a team I really wanted to sign for but they were in the old fourth division (now known as football League Two) at the time and maybe my heart was ruling my head a little bit.*
>
> *One Sunday morning I was approached by the scout at Manchester United and they offered me a week's trial; and it came to the end of the week and they came back with schoolboy forms that would have taken me up to 16, but with no guarantee of receiving an apprenticeship. I also had an offer to go on trial at Everton a week after the Manchester United trial.*
>
> *I told United I was going to train with Everton because there was an opportunity to work with Gordon Banks who was doing the goalkeeping at the time. From that, Manchester United came back to me and said they didn't want me to go to Everton and consequently offered me a two year apprenticeship and it started from there really.*
>
> *It was a lot different back then compared to what it's like now."*
>
> **Mike Pollitt - Wigan Athletic FC**

"I went off to university in Liverpool and it wasn't until I was 21 that I got my first trial at Millwall. That went well and I was offered my first professional contract at 21.

For me it was different, when you are in an academy they try to condition the lads for professional football; you are being monitored, taught different aspects to look after your body, and given advice on what to eat.

I went from university to football, and with the nightlife attached to university, I probably wasn't in the best physical shape I could be in. I went to Millwall and the first six months I was at the club were a huge culture shock to me. I'd been playing local football in Jersey at an amateur level and I had to adapt to playing professionally, so I was put on diets and fitness programmes to condition myself to play professional football. I had to build myself up, gain my core strength, improve my stamina, and all that sort of stuff."

Peter Vincenti - Rochdale AFC

"I was scouted aged 15, playing for my local side: Croydon Athletic. We were doing well in the Kent League and we had a few scouts that came to watch us play.

One of them was a former manager in our league and he was scouting for West Ham, so it was all set up for me to go there on a six-week trial at the end of season. But, before that happened, Crystal Palace came up, so I thought I'd go there, and if nothing came out of it, I could go and try my luck at West Ham at the end of season. Luckily after three weeks or so, on trial at Crystal Palace, they wanted to sign me up for the under 16's academy team. I couldn't refuse, even though I had a trial pending at the end of season, it was something I couldn't rely on, so I gladly signed."

Matt Parsons - Plymouth Argyle FC

Chapter 1

You are on trial

However a player is spotted, there will almost always be a trial period involved somewhere along the process, and there's one of two ways you can approach a trial or selection day:

1. Play it safe
2. Do something out of the ordinary to catch the eye

Both approaches carry a risk element. If you play it too safe, just play the simple ball and don't impose yourself on the game, you could be seen as someone who wouldn't improve the team and someone who may not stand out in a competitive trial environment.

Alternatively if you do try something out of the ordinary, it's easy to do *too much* and constantly lose the ball, or be seen as an individual and not a team player. Ultimately there is no rule of thumb here; it depends on the clubs' and scouts/coaches' approach, and the type of player they are looking for on any given day.

There wouldn't be any harm in asking the scout/coach what they expect from you in your respective position before your trial begins; the clarity of the answer given may leave you a little wiser (or maybe not) as to how you approach the trial.

However, there are things that can help improve your chances of a favourable outcome. For instance, it's recommended that you 'have a voice' and make yourself known, are willing to talk in the dressing room, mingle with fellow players, and make yourself comfortable in your surroundings. This will help with confidence and allow you to feel happy within a club environment. If you're happy - that usually reflects in your game and allows you to play at your best.

Controlling nerves and playing 'the game', not the occasion, will give you the best possible chance to showcase your full footballing ability.

It's important not to dwell on your mistakes. In turn, get your head around the fact that you *will* make mistakes, *even the best players in the world make mistakes*. You will be out of position and you will give the ball away sometimes, it's inevitable. It's the way you react to these mistakes that will define you as a footballer, and a positive reaction to making a mistake will impress managers and go a long way to helping you gain that contract or be selected to join a club academy.

If you begin to dwell on your mistakes - your confidence will drop. This can quickly spiral into a collection of errors that can damage your chance of being signed for a club.

> *"I know how nerve-wracking it can be in the lead up to a trial - the night before in bed, and the day of the trial on the way there in the car. All I tried to do was think positive because positive thoughts lead to positive outcomes. I used to picture myself running down the wing putting in crosses, tackling well.*
>
> *I think one of the main things is not to dwell on mistakes; everyone makes them, nobody's perfect. It's mainly how you react to these mistakes that defines you as a player, one bad pass isn't the end of the world. I can't remember coming through a game without making a mistake or thinking to myself I should have done better.*
>
> *Lots of coaches don't look at the mistake half the time, it's your reaction and how you are after you've given the ball away, or scored an own goal, for instance. Are you the type to shy away or are you the type who wants to get on the ball, get over it and show your ability? The latter is definitely the way to be!"*
>
> **Matt Parsons - Plymouth Argyle FC**

Be strong in mind as well as in body

The first 15 minutes of a match are vital for any footballer; it can dictate the remainder of your game, leading to a great (or very poor) performance.

Usually football is played over 90 minutes so you have plenty of time - when it's going wrong - to get yourself back on track; back to performing at your best. Unfortunately with the number of lads taking part in academy trial days you may only have 15-20 minutes to shine as they need to take a look at a large number of players, so you will need to get over any mistakes very quickly.

If you can show your mental strength so that negative actions - like giving a penalty away - don't affect your overall game, that's a huge positive. With the demands and pressures that are part of being a modern day professional footballer, it has never been more important to be mentally strong. It is something that most coaches will look for when considering a player for selection.

It's a dog eat dog industry

Another essential thing to take on board is that when you enter a competitive environment, such as a trial or an academy, it can be difficult to form *real* friendships as ultimately you have the same goals as the other lads, and will be competing against everyone else to earn that contract. Sometimes, you have to be willing to tread on toes to look after your own best interests.

"There was a young keeper at United, he was the main man and had been there since he was seven or something, and he was a good keeper and was the number 1. So I went there and blew him out of the water in training; every session I'd be eating the work up, and working myself into the ground and he couldn't hack it. My dad would always tell me, "If you're hurting, don't show it. While he lies on the floor you stand up and walk past him." Mind games at that age!

It eventually wore him down and after four weeks of me being there he quit and I went on from there really."

Ben Amos - Manchester United FC

Making it into a pro club is just the start

Even if you become part of a professional club, footballers are constantly in a shop window looking to progress and play at the highest standard they possibly can.

> *"At the age of 14 I was fortunate to have the opportunity to move to Bolton Wanderers. I was playing for Bristol City at the time and enjoying my football but having the chance to move to Premier League Bolton was a chance I couldn't miss out on."*
>
> **Chris Stokes - Forest Green Rovers FC**

Advancing to gain your first full time professional contract doesn't mean you can relax; your career is a changing landscape full of opportunities that can allow you to move up the leagues, or drop down the leagues just as easily. The direction you will go depends on your *attitude* towards the game. Football should not just be considered a hobby it should become a healthy obsession!

The most successful people are obsessed with the subject they are involved with. Richard Branson is successful in business because he is obsessed with business. Obsession shouldn't make you unwell or prevent you from sleeping, but you should be obsessed enough to work at your goals tirelessly. That is what you've got to do to become a professional footballer. You need to be willing to run through brick walls to achieve your goal. At times you'll need to be ruthless and tell (and possibly upset) those closest to you to take a step back if you feel they are proving detrimental to your progression.

Complacency is your enemy

Whatever level you play your football at, ensure you don't become complacent and take anything for granted as this can easily and quickly result in you dropping down the leagues, and even falling out of the game altogether.

> *"I'm 34 and have been in the professional game for nearly 20 years but I still stay after training and work on aspects of my game that I feel I'm struggling with. If I'm not happy with my game and my form dips I want to get back to where I want to be, and I'm willing to do whatever it takes to get there. You have to be willing to work on your game every day and it doesn't matter if you're someone looking to get noticed or someone, like me, who has been playing professional football for nearly 20 years."*
>
> **Guy Branston (co-author) - a personal reflection**

Chapter 1

How much do you want it?

"I deal with a lot of players that claim they want to become a footballer. But are they willing to travel halfway across the country for a one day trial? Will they do whatever it takes to make their dream a reality? In my experience, I would estimate that 80% of those players that have claimed they strive to become a professional wouldn't.

A lot of players sit around, boast about their footballing talent, and talk a good game - but don't back it up on the pitch. People try to act like a professional footballer without actually being a footballer and a great example of this is the local player that picks up £30-£40 a game and walks around with a certain aura as though they have made it. Unfortunately they haven't. This is not to say they are not good enough to step up but you have to prove you're good enough and this is where the hard work comes in. You have to be willing to take risks and grasp every opportunity that presents itself.

It comes down to asking yourself what you want out of life. A lot of lads across the country say they want to become a footballer, but do you really want to become a footballer? Are you willing to make that last ditch tackle knowing you could take a whack? Will you take that clattering from the goalkeeper to score a goal that could be the difference between winning and drawing? Are you willing to spend hours in your garden working on your touch to make yourself that little bit better than everyone else? Are you willing to do that extra sprint or extra gym work after training? Are you prepared to do whatever it takes to get that professional contract?

I know I was certainly ready to do whatever it takes and it brought its rewards. I do extra work that will benefit me on the pitch because I know for a fact that if I put the hard work in, I will get my rewards."

Guy Branston (co-author) - a personal reflection

Summary

Make no mistake - stepping on to the footballing ladder is just the start of a very physical and mentally demanding career that requires maximum commitment and effort with no guarantee of success. The percentage of lads that make a living in the game is very low.

Here are the top tips from this chapter:

- At a trial, you need to do something memorable to help get yourself noticed.
- Play the game not the occasion.
- Don't dwell on mistakes, everyone will make them.
- A positive reaction to mistakes will impress scouts/managers and coaches.
- Don't let comments regarding your physical attributes stop you from striving to achieve your dream.
- Football should become a healthy obsession not just a hobby.
- Actions speak louder than words; don't just say you want to become a professional footballer, prove it!

2

Prepare to Make Sacrifices

As you tread the path to professional football, there will be numerous sacrifices you have to make to give yourself the best possible opportunities to progress and flourish in the beautiful game.

Sacrifices are difficult to take at any age but when you need to make these sacrifices from a young age – they can be a lot harder to deal with. Often, they require individuals to grow up a lot faster than other kids of a similar age.

Get packing, it's time to leave home

One of the biggest and hardest sacrifices to make is leaving home. If you have the mentality and drive to do whatever it takes to become a footballer, then you need to be flexible and willing to move away from the area you have grown up in. If a meaningful opportunity presents itself, it might mean leaving friends, family and loved ones behind. This is not to say that moving away from 'what you know' is a bad thing. It can help you develop both as a footballer and as a person.

"When I went away to university it was always with the intention of returning to Jersey. I had a job lined up on the Island in the finance industry. I was then offered the trial at Millwall and consequently signed professionally for them.

It was a very different feeling being away from the Island professionally than it was as a student and I found it more difficult as I wasn't to know when I was going back to the Island.

Now, as I've moved on, got a little older, I've become a lot more comfortable. In fact if you were to ask me today, if I'd go back to Jersey, the answer would probably be no. But, at the time, it was difficult moving away from family and friends who subconsciously I was looking forward to seeing after my three years at university."

Peter Vincenti - Rochdale AFC

"I made it into the national school at Lilleshall which was one of the best things that could have happened to me, and also the first genuine tale of sacrifice as I was required to leave home and board there for the final two years of my school life.

Alan Smith was in my year but he only lasted three months as he couldn't deal with living away from home; despite this he went on to achieve great things. It was a great experience and was where I truly matured as a player and a person but I only got home every three weeks for a weekend and every school holiday so it wasn't easy."

Kevin Nicholson - Torquay United FC

"I left home at 16, and started off at Portsmouth. I was up at 6:30 getting the train into the station and then riding down to the ground from there. Once I arrived I started my jobs at 8:30-9:00 every morning, we had a lot of jobs to do; I had to sort out 10 blokes' kits, I had a van to clean, had a boot room to keep clean, we did the pitch, we did the terraces, a whole multitude of things to do."

Steve Claridge - Former Leicester, Portsmouth, Birmingham & Others

Football clubs are constantly on the lookout for top footballing talent. As the game has grown, and developed, so has the investment in football clubs' scouting networks. This means clubs generally have a lot more scouts than they've ever had, covering greater areas of the UK and even globally (if budgets permit). If you are making a name for yourself in the local press, there's a good chance local clubs will be made aware of your talent before clubs from further afield become aware. So you don't necessarily need to leave home.

The real shop window starts when you are playing for your local academy, travelling up and down the country, competing and excelling against other academy sides. Offers will then be put on the table and it's likely some will be from clubs outside the area; it is then up to you to decide what the best footballing move might be, regardless of location.

If you move away, there is a good chance you will live full time with local families who have affiliations with your new club. You will, however, still have opportunities to see your family if you are given time off or don't have a fixture on certain weekends.

"I've had to make a number of big decisions and sacrifices in my life. The biggest one was at the age of 14 when I was fortunate to have the opportunity to move to Bolton Wanderers. I was playing for Bristol City at the time and enjoying my football but having the chance to move to Premier League Bolton was a chance I couldn't miss out on. I discussed the decision a lot with my family and in the end we all agreed I should go.

It happened really quickly and looking back on it now I didn't really realise what I had got myself into. Moving four hours away from my family as a 14 year old was tough. I had to grow up really quickly and learn to look after myself from such a young age. It was a huge life change from what I was used to - living at home - but was a great experience and it made me the person I am today."

Chris Stokes - Forest Green Rovers FC

There are a lot of players who are not willing to make that sacrifice - they find the idea of leaving the area they grew up in daunting. Moving away can make you realise who is important in your life, because your friends who want to stay in touch will make the effort to do so, and the rest won't bother making time for you.

Whilst leaving home and travelling around the country to live in a different area is a big sacrifice, some players make a much bigger sacrifice and move to a different country to help open doors and present themselves with greater opportunities. For some, a massive culture shock can be felt.

In the UK, there are plenty of international young footballers who come over to English clubs at 14 or 15 years of age and live with local families, with different traditions, a different cuisine, and different daily routines. Take a moment to think about how 'big a deal' this might be for someone from the other side of the world. They have made a choice to give themselves the best possible chance to succeed.

The foreign players that tend to cope with this transition the best are those that embrace the culture, start to learn the language, and really try to integrate themselves in the community. In other words, they embrace their new world. The same advice is relevant to British players – embrace your new environment!

"I was born on the beautiful island of Bermuda. Great weather, friendly people and amazing beaches! From a very young age I had always told people that I wanted to be a professional footballer in England.

In order for me to move to England I had to make a deal with my parents. The deal was that if I had attained seven GCSEs grade C and above, then we would move to England. For me it was the chance of a lifetime. I knew what I had to do in order to - at least - be given the chance to chase my dream."

Jonte Smith - Crawley Town FC

Friends come and go

"Along the footballing road you will make, and lose, many friends. I, personally, have lost touch with many mates, and to be honest this came as a result of me being selfish. It was a selfishness to succeed in life, selfishness to improve my life and get to where I wanted to be, and that target was to be a professional footballer at the highest level I could achieve. That's where I had to make sacrifices."

Guy Branston (co-author) - a personal reflection

Choosing and maintaining friends throughout the footballing journey is a difficult process. As with all walks of life you'll find that a lot of friends you have from childhood won't be your friends in the future – even with email, Facebook, BBM, and other social networking platforms. Many friendship bonds will break along the way. But these changes are an important learning curve; the friends that stick with you through thick and thin are there for a reason and are likely to be there for the rest of your life.

The problem is that football is such a sought-after career, and appeals to the majority of young lads growing up, so jealousy comes into play when they see you making a success of yourself.

"I had a best mate that I grew up with, and he was a good footballer - a lot better than me on the ball. He was a really nice kid to me when we were growing up, and as soon as I signed onto YTS at Leicester he changed. Everything was more negative towards me: he wanted me to get caught out, he wanted me to get drunk with him, and he wasn't supportive. The supporting element had gone and this was from my so-called best mate from school who I had fond memories of hanging around with.

It took me a long time to realise - I was about 25, so after nine years of friendship - that this lad was holding me back and was becoming a destructive element within my life. As soon as I cut him out things went from strength to strength."

Guy Branston (co-author) - a personal reflection

If your so-called mates are happy when you are losing, or being dropped from the squad, and enjoy seeing you fail, these are the types of people you don't really want to be associated with; they can destroy your morale and self-belief.

For every friend you lose there will be someone in your life that gives you the inspiration and drive to kick on and make something of yourself.

Besides your friends from home, those you have grown up with, you always have a chance to make friends within the football clubs you are at, not always 'best friends' - as it is such a competitive and cut-throat industry, with everyone out to look after their own best interests – but good friends nonetheless.

As you might imagine, the further your career develops and the more successful you become you will find everyone wants to be your friend and benefit from the nice things that come as part and parcel of being a footballer. You need to ask yourself 'are they my friends because of who I am as a person?' or 'do they only want to know me because of what I do for a living?'

It's a harsh reality (but something that you need to realise and act upon very swiftly) - if you are to be successful there are certain people you need to cut out of your life as they can be detrimental and hinder your chances of achieving your goals. These can include the so-called friends who encourage you to miss training, put unfair pressure on you to take up bad habits, mock you for putting football first (staying in the night before a match rather than heading to late night house parties), and friends who enjoy seeing you slip up.

Stay focused and keep your eye on the prize

If you are looking to become a footballer your focus and determination must be channelled to help you become the best you can be. This will generally mean you miss out on certain events growing up (to some degree) and maybe not encounter the same childhood experiences as non-footballers. But if you manage to accomplish what you set out to do, none of that will matter and you will have no regrets.

As you grow up there will be times when people try to divert your attention and get you into bad habits that can veer you off course. When you reach the age of 18, when alcohol, gambling, cigarettes (and even drugs to some extent) become accessible, it can be difficult to not be swayed. Especially if you're around people that are getting involved with those sorts of things.

Young adulthood is a time when companies (alcohol, lifestyle products, etc.) look to get hold of you and take advantage of your vulnerability. You need to be stubborn and avoid temptation, as it can have unfavourable effects on your development and hugely reduce your chances of progressing in the game.

"The biggest sacrifice for me (and this is where I feel a lot of boys fall off) was when you get to that age of 13, 14 maybe 15 at school, and your friends start going to school parties and house parties, staying up late. As they get older drink starts to creep in. I didn't go for any of that, so I did feel that was a bit of a sacrifice.

The kids would try to make fun of me at school the next day for not going, 'Where were you last night? Why do you never come to the parties?' and I did really want to go. But, from an early age, my Dad was always in my ear reminding me that if you start going down that line, that is when your football will start to suffer and your dedication to football will also suffer."

Matt Piper - Former Leicester City FC & Sunderland AFC

"I was never at a pro club when I was younger; I played non- league football until I was 21 so I was always living at home. My friends were going out, drinking and partying.

For me it was a case of what do I want? Did I want to go out and do all that with them, and enjoy that life for a few years? Or did I want to work hard and make something of the talent in football that I had? So I sacrificed going out and kind of enjoying being young."

Craig Mackail-Smith - Brighton & Hove Albion FC

Think about this from the perspective of a football club. It does not matter how good you may be – if you have an alcohol problem, or smoke cigarettes, the club won't see you as having the 'professional mindset' needed to maintain your career at the highest level. Clubs are unwilling to invest in players who cannot control themselves, or players who fail to deliver performances week-in and week-out because of outside influences.

Clubs need to think about the needs of the whole organisation and all the players; they do not like disruptive forces that can negatively influence their other players (who are seen as investments). If you have a drinking problem and end up dragging your colleagues into it – the club will soon get rid of you to save the others.

"When I was living at home I was growing up in a society where many of my friends had house parties for their 17th and 18th birthdays. However, I had to say 'no' to most of these parties as they were held on weekends, a time I dedicated purely to football training and matches. This was a choice I took upon myself, but I did witness some of my talented peers going to these events even when they had fixtures the next day. None of them made pro…"

Jack Baldwin - Peterborough United FC

"I've always been quite disciplined in training and stuff. Your friends do try and lead you astray and you hear of so many great young players at 16/17/18 who get involved with the lure of drinking, girls and stuff like that. I was always the one, when I was out, who would say, "I have a game tomorrow I've got to head back home." It's the sacrifices you have to make at that age.

You get to the age of 17/18 and you are able to go into the pub and get a drink and stuff like that. Don't get me wrong I had the odd drink but I never drank excessively like some do at that age. I might have had the odd night out here and there but I was pretty regimented. I believed football was much more important.

My friends who were not going on to play football would go out but it's a sacrifice you have to make. At a club like Manchester United, where Alex Ferguson was in charge, it was quite disciplined all the way down into the youth teams, so you couldn't do it. You would stand out like a sore thumb if you were going out and drinking, it just wasn't acceptable really."

Mike Pollitt - Wigan Athletic FC

It helps if you have the right people around you giving support. It is important to have friends and family that realise you have a talent and, as a result, don't try to put pressure on you to do anything that may prevent that talent being rewarded.

"I didn't really have a problem going out and stuff like that; I was lucky I had decent friends around me. Kids always try and push their luck and get carried away with themselves a little bit, but I had that slapped out of me, not literally slapped out of me, I've got to state that! But we've always had a tight knit family and a lot of lads don't have that. So I have to say I'm lucky in that sense.

My advice would be to surround yourself with people who are going to help get you where you want to be, not hold you back."

Ben Amos - Manchester United FC

"My closest friends were really good; they understood what I was sacrificing and why I was doing it. They never really pressured me and would always support me and see how I was getting on, and were interested in how well I was doing.

Other friends around me wanted me to always come out, and they wanted to try and break me and would try making me drink. So there were different friends doing different things."

Craig Mackail-Smith - Brighton & Hove Albion FC

You are what you eat

Another consideration is nutrition, ensuring you are living right *and eating right* is very important. Adapting your diet usually requires giving up, or at least vastly cutting down, on some of your favourite foods; swapping a McDonalds for rice, vegetables and chicken. Again, we are talking about sacrifice.

Doing what you need to do, in all aspects of your life, to give yourself the best chance of footballing stardom.

Studying and understanding nutrition from an early age is important. You want to get your body in a condition to play at your best level in one of the most competitive industries out there. Looking after your body properly can give you a head start and allow you to compete for longer at a higher intensity.

"Another sacrifice is watching what you eat. At the time, and we're talking the mid 90's, the information we received wasn't too in-depth on nutrition."

Matt Piper - Former Leicester City FC & Sunderland AFC

Summary

What you sacrifice depends on how strong your drive is to pursue a career as a professional footballer. This will be a key factor in whether you make it or not. Ask yourself *why* you want to be a footballer, and then establish how badly you want it. What are you prepared to give up and sacrifice to make it?

We are not saying if you give up all the negative things 'you will be successful' and achieve your dream but you'll give yourself a much stronger chance to succeed.

Success doesn't come without a degree of sacrifice; any successful footballer will tell you they had to make sacrifices along the way, no matter how good their natural footballing talent was.

Top tips from this chapter:

- Be willing to relocate if it's best for your personal football development.
- Friends will come and go but don't let this worry you or affect your drive to succeed in the game.
- Don't be misguided or misled; stay focused on what you want to achieve.
- Healthy eating can help give you the edge.
- To be successful you have to expect to make sacrifices.

3

Put in the Hours and You'll Reap the Rewards

If you want a shot at the big time - hard work is the key. No player is perfect and (as the saying goes) *you get out what you put in*. With the global pool of talent, and the competitive nature of the industry, footballers have to work harder than ever to get their chance. Don't waste it; get your head down, put in the hours, and see where it takes you.

With football being so competitive, it is essential you take it upon yourself to go that extra mile and commit yourself to lots of training. This should include on and off the field training and you should be aiming to get yourself in the best possible shape: physically, technically, and mentally.

"I think it is key that you do a lot on your own. If you're at a full time club you've got to take a lot of the onus onto yourself. Coaches have got so many boys to look after; they can't have your individual wellbeing at the front of their mind all the time. They have a lot to deal with. I think you've got to take a lot of it on yourself - in terms of your own progression and improvement."

Neill Collins - Sheffield United FC

Chapter 3

Adopt the right attitude

Having the right attitude and work ethic towards training, as well as fully applying yourself, will allow you to become the best footballer you can be.

> *"I have always worked as hard as I can work. I've always put 100% in and go all out, I stay behind after training and do a lot of stuff off my own back because I want to be the best and I want to achieve what I want to achieve. And the only way to do that is to work as hard as possible."*
>
> **Craig Mackail-Smith - Brighton & Hove Albion FC**

Without the right attitude you will struggle to keep pace with the players around you who *are willing* to put in the effort to improve themselves in every aspect of the game. If you don't make the effort you will find, over time, that you're not developing or progressing at the same speed as other players within the squad. Ultimately, this could result in you failing to make an impact with the team you are in, and potentially being released by the club.

Get yourself in the right frame of mind and adopt the right attitude, as this will give you the perfect platform to make the most of every opportunity that presents itself.

> *"For me I would say the determination and hours you put in training is down to the desire of the individual.*
>
> *A lot of people don't believe this when I say it, but I grew up with a lot of people who were very good at football but who didn't actually love the game.*
>
> *You get certain kids who want to watch football whenever it's on, play it at every given chance they get: in the living room, out the front of their house, in the back garden and at school. There were quite a lot of really good players that I grew up with who didn't watch it, didn't go home and play it, and who were more interested in playing computer games. But I was one of those kids that absolutely loved the game, so I spent hours and hours and hours practicing and playing football, but that was because I loved it."*
>
> **Matt Piper - Former Leicester City FC & Sunderland AFC**

On the training field

When you are training, make sure you are familiar with what the manager expects of you and what your role within the training session is. This can go a long way to catching the manager's eye as consistency is a key factor when selecting players. If you're working harder than other players in the same position and you're doing your job week-in week-out, it is difficult for that to go unnoticed, making you hard to forget.

"Some days you go to training and, naturally, you feel tired, lethargic, and maybe even stressed with things in your life at that time. But I used to think if I went to training and I'm not putting the effort in, someone in Norway or another kid in Spain will be putting the required effort in, and when we get to whatever age he will be ahead of me."

Ben Amos - Manchester United FC

Managers will always try to dictate how you play and mould you to how they want you to perform. This may involve playing out of position or playing a style of football you don't feel comfortable with. Nevertheless you must knuckle down and do that specific job for the team and the manager or game time may be hard to come by.

Again, this is where adopting the right attitude is very important. If you're asked to play out of position *just do it* for the team. If you are the type of player to throw your arms around and sulk, when asked to play out of position, it's very unlikely you'll make it in the professional game.

Where possible, try and be true to yourself; if your style of play is that of a ball playing midfielder, be a ball playing midfielder in training and play to your strengths. If you don't best utilize the footballing attributes you have, but try to be a type of player you're not, it's likely your performance levels will drop dramatically, decreasing the chance of you giving the best account of yourself.

If you think you can offer the team a lot more in a certain position or by playing in a certain style then have a constructive conversation with the manager. The majority of managers want you to *communicate* and if you're really not happy -

make them aware. Be aware, though, there is a time and a place. Try to do this in a professional manner and in the correct environment.

It is becoming increasingly difficult to cement a fixed position within a team because of the way the modern game is developing. There seems to be a trend with managers and clubs where they are looking for utility players who can play in numerous positions. *Versatility* can make you a very valuable asset to a team! The problem, though, is that it becomes difficult to develop into a complete player in a specific position as positional and technical requirements vary so much between different positions. It is challenging to dedicate the required time to practice and focus on all the different aspects that come with playing in a number of positions. In spite of the challenges, being versatile can work in your favour; being able to play a variety of positions gives you a much greater chance of making the starting 11 and prolonging your stay at a club.

Out of hours

It is easier to train hard under the guidance of a manager or a coach who encourages, motivates, and pushes you to work hard. However, away from the training ground is where you will really notice yourself progressing more rapidly than those players who just train then go home.

It's something you should continue even after receiving a contract and playing in the professional game; it can be difficult as a young lad coming through as you can be seen as 'busy' and receive banter from more experienced players within the dressing room. However, the really hard working players continue to work after training hours and can excel beyond those around them. Look at what

Cristiano Ronaldo achieved whilst at Manchester United through having a burning desire and willingness to put in the extra work to improve every aspect of his game and physical performance.

"When I became a pro, that's when I let myself down a little bit. A lot of people do this. You have older people in the team - and they just train, have a quick shower, a bit of dinner, and then go - and when you make it, you want to fit in with the first team. The banter, between footballers, can go something like, "Look at him staying behind, he's so busy." That gets bandied around a lot and it's said in quite a negative way. So once you have reached that level and have reached the goal of becoming a professional footballer it's easy to fall into that trap. I did fall into the trap and definitely didn't train as much as I could have done."

Matt Piper - Former Leicester City FC & Sunderland AFC

"I wouldn't say I stayed behind at training. What I would say is, if I felt I hadn't done enough then I would always go and do extra. However working hard isn't the only remedy to being fit. Some people are naturally fit and I was one of them: I have never been beaten in a long distance race. I then got to a point where I wasn't really living properly; I'd never really prepared properly. I got to about 26 and if you don't live properly, it begins to catch up with you.

I couldn't beat a kiddie called Steve Welsh (who had just come out the army) in a race and I'd never been beaten in long distance running. So I went down to Blandford Army camp for Cambridge and that was the first time I had three square meals (Breakfast, Lunch and Dinner), I trained three times and I actually lived right, slept right and did it properly. And at the end of that I beat this kid and broke the army record.

I then thought to myself; what is the difference in me, between the Sunday when I came here and the Sunday when I left? Obviously it was that I trained and lived properly. From that day on I changed my whole lifestyle and completely changed it around and that's the reason I was able to play almost 1200 games.

My eating habits and everything I do now is totally for my own well-being and fitness. I also believe: the fitter you are the less likely you are to get injured."

Steve Claridge - Former Leicester, Portsmouth, Birmingham & Others

---

> *"Even now, at 42, with training I like to do a bit extra. When I started at United we got to training quite early after catching the bus so we would head to the gym and use the indoor facilities and Astroturf pitches.*
>
> *I would always work on little things like my kicking and handling to try and improve that a little bit.*
>
> *I'm still at Wigan and I try get there early in the morning. I'm usually the first to arrive and the last to leave. It's something that was instilled in me from an early age and it's something that has kept me going in the game."*
>
> **Mike Pollitt - Wigan Athletic FC**

> *"I still do extra training, extra shooting and things outside of football. It's the little things that can give you that added edge.*
>
> *For me I want to stay on top of everything, and I feel if I'm working really hard, working my body and working on the technical side of things, then I'm getting better and I'm feeling confident when I go out onto the football pitch.*
>
> *I think it's something that has been inbuilt in me, coming from non-league where it's not the most technical of leagues; the only way of creating something or getting anything out of the game is by working hard and I think that's how I've always gone through my career.*
>
> *I just try and work as hard as I can in a game and treat it as if it was my last, so I just run my body into the ground."*
>
> **Craig Mackail-Smith - Brighton & Hove Albion**

There are many additional exercises and activities you can do outside of football that can really help your overall game on the pitch, anything from yoga to training with a running club can have really positive effects on your level of performance and rate of progression.

"I used to do taekwondo, two nights a week. My Dad and I used to go and my cousin joined us as well. That was hard cardio and flexibility as well as a lot of stretching and I'm quite flexible now because of that. I think it kind of helped with my mechanics. In football a lot of it is your efficiency, how you move, and getting from A to B as quickly and efficiently as possible. I did semi-contact sparring and circuit training and I imagine that has helped with my condition now."

Ben Amos - Manchester United FC

"When I was 14/15, I started going to a local athletics club. I used to train with my boys' clubs twice a week and still go to the athletics club once or twice a week as well. That improved me so much in terms of my fitness and things like that. On top of that I tried to do the weights as much as I could, but at that age you're still not really able to do heavy lifting. But I did what I could."

Neill Collins - Sheffield United FC

"I was also undertaking training of my own, some evenings, when I had any spare time. This involved going for a run, taking a football to the local playing grounds, individual strength training (press-ups, sit-ups, squats). In general, I spent a lot of time on my own, with a football."

Jack Baldwin - Peterborough United FC

"In my spare time I often went to the gym to get that one step ahead of everyone else, and to get fitter. That's just how I was."

Matt Parsons - Plymouth Argyle FC

Chapter 3

It is vital to develop your technique, no matter what position you play, as this will transform you into a better all-round player. There are many talented players out there but no one is faultless in every single aspect of their game. *Identify your weaknesses* and practice, practice, practice.

> *"Stay determined and all the hard work will pay off. As long as you practice, practice and practice some more. Really try to hone your skills. You will know yourself what your strengths are but work on your weaknesses as there is no better time than when you're young to turn those weaknesses into your strengths."*
>
> **Chris Smalling - Manchester United FC**

Identify what is required in the position you play and work on every aspect, from the technical and physical demands of that position to your starting position and overall positional awareness. Work with other players who are also willing to put in additional hours, and create patterns of play and real life game scenarios. Run through different patterns of play at different speeds, using different techniques. You will be better equipped to flourish when you are confronted with the game scenario you've worked on… when it really matters and points are at stake.

In time you will find you become more accomplished, whether that's working on your first touch, heading or shooting. There is simply *no getting away* from the fact that the only way to improve is to spend hours on the training field working on your technique. Granted, this can be a very frustrating process, but in time you will see the benefits and enjoy your football more as you will find you're a more complete and dominant player.

Study football as a subject

Training is not required only for the physical and technical sides of the game. It will be hugely beneficial to train your brain by studying the nutritional, tactical and mental side to things. It's important you embrace all aspects of football and have a great passion and interest for football as a subject. Understanding all aspects will not only help you get into professional football, but could also help extend your career in the game once there.

"I've looked into every aspect of health, diet, fitness, and psychology, to prolong and improve my career and I'm still playing at 33 coming up to 600 games. I'm a huge believer in going after your dreams and learning all you can along the way."

Kevin Nicholson - Torquay United FC

Reading and researching managerial manuals will help you understand the tactical side of the game; this will improve your reading of the game, help you defend against opposition movements, and help you identify danger more quickly. These resources will also offer insights into the offensive side of the game allowing you to create space for yourself making you a more prominent and influential player.

Studying nutrition and understanding what foods should (and shouldn't) be part of your everyday diet is very useful, as careful diet planning, along with fitness training, will allow you to train harder, more regularly, and for longer. In fact, the combination of healthy eating and healthy living could give you the competitive edge to gain a professional contract over your footballing peers. It demonstrates commitment!

Training your brain and reading self-help books is a great way to get yourself in the right mental state to encourage positive thinking. Positive thinking and confidence are key areas for dealing with the pressure that you are put under throughout the footballing journey.

Nullifying negative emotions suffered as a result of anxiety is very important and when performances start to suffer you need to bring yourself back into a positive state of mind. A lot of worry stems from the unknowns of the future. Make the most of now and enjoy it.

In sport psychology – there is talk about 'controlling the controllables'. In other words, you cannot control the state of the pitch, the weather, the size of the opposition – so do not worry about them! Instead, focus on the things you can control such as work rate, communication, and staying positive. As long as you fully apply yourself and put maximum effort into everything you do, then you gain huge respect. You can be proud of yourself as you have done everything *in your power* to do the best you can.

Good time management will help

As you move through life there will obviously be other commitments that require your time, whether that is education, family commitments, or something else. Good organisation and time management are essential to enable you to practice the required amount to ensure you stay at the top of your game, In other words, outside activities and events in your life will have to be *prioritized*.

It is likely you will have to let people down in order to give yourself the best chance of fulfilling a long and successful career in the game. If you have to let people down, *do it properly*; give them plenty of warning and an explanation as necessary. We talked, in Chapter 2, about the importance of a good support network. You want people to encourage and help you on your footballing path, so treat them with respect and courtesy. For example, if you fail to turn up to a meeting without any explanation, you might damage that person's respect for you and maybe (over the longer term) their support for you.

Summary

The amount of work you put in, on and off the field, will depend on your attitude and how deep your desire and passion to succeed in the game is. It is really easy to *say* you want to become a professional footballer but you have to mean it and be willing to dedicate a huge amount of your time to football. If you mean it, show it!

Like most things in life - *you get out what you put in*; all those additional hours training might seem like slow progress (even a waste of time) but you will begin to see noticeable benefits. It may take weeks, months, or even years - but be patient and stay positive. A dedication to your sport is the only way you have any chance of making it.

"A lot of academies now say, and it has some scientific proof from a study that was carried out in America, that for anyone to make it as a professional sportsman or woman - they are required to dedicate 10,000 hours to meaningful practice. That can be under the guidance of a coach or playing in the back garden on your own."

Matt Piper - Former Leicester City FC & Sunderland AFC

Top tips from this chapter:

- Employ the correct attitude, keep focused on your ultimate goal and put in the hard work to drive towards it.
- Listen to your manager and play how he wants you to play; the manager picks the team and you want to be part of it.
- Identify your position specific weaknesses (even write them down in a notebook) and spend hours practicing to improve your technique.
- Be intrinsically motivated to take it upon yourself to practice and work hard away from the training ground.
- Dedicate time to studying and understanding the different aspects of football.
- Good organisation should help you identify the times you can dedicate to football.
- Communicate with people in your support network; do not leave them in the lurch.

4

Stay Focused throughout your Footballing Journey

Being in the right frame of mind is just as important as getting your body in the right shape; they fit hand in hand. Without the right focus you'll find it difficult to motivate yourself to put in the physical work required to get as far in the game as you can.

If suitable set yourself challenging goals to strive for

You need to be very narrow-minded and ensure you're not swayed from reaching your ultimate goal; a strict regimented routine will put you in good stead. Target what you want to achieve, and *set goals* along the way to give yourself something to strive for. This can be anything from what club and level you'd like to play at, to making the starting line-up, or even representing your country.

Specific goals and targets will help you to stay focused and help give you the determination, drive, and motivation to progress and reach the ultimate goals you set yourself. Goals can be reassessed at various stages throughout your personal footballing journey. To begin with - aim high. Why not reach for the stars?

However goal setting isn't for everyone. If you are someone who becomes demoralised and upset if initial goals and targets are not reached, then it's probably a good idea to just work as hard as you can and see where it takes you. Whether you set goals and targets depends on how you are as a person and what method serves best to motivate and get the best out of you.

"I didn't really self talk and set targets as I personally feel if you start to set targets then you start to disappoint yourself.

I would never go out and think I was going to score, and I never went out and thought I was going to have a good game. I just went out, and if I ran around, and I did what I knew I had to do, then that would be enough and anything else on top of that would be a bonus.

The problem with setting targets is that you worry about achieving those targets; you put yourself under more pressure and that can, in some cases, affect your game. In a football sense I never set myself any targets, however my aim was always to be as fit, strong and as well prepared as I could be. In a sense they were my targets, but they were personal and not football specific targets.

I was at Birmingham and there was a lad that came in and took my place and he said "Steve Claridge is a good player, but he didn't score the goals that I'm going to score."

I looked at it and thought let's just wait and see. For Birmingham I think I scored 28 one year and the year I left I'd scored 14 up until Christmas. I think he ended up with two that year. I think you set yourself up for a fall by saying things like that."

Steve Claridge - Former Leicester, Portsmouth, Birmingham & Others

---

You cannot afford to lose focus

Focus is something you need to keep at all stages in your career. In fact, you should try and remain focused for every minute of every game, training session, and team talk. You cannot allow your mind to wander. In a match situation, for example, switching off for even a few seconds can allow your opponent to steal a yard on you and result in your team conceding a goal.

> *"Concentration is one of the big factors that can be the difference in you scoring that final chance in a game or making that last ditch tackle. Being able to stay focused for the whole duration of the training session or game will really help you stand out from the crowd. When you master that, you will have the consistency in your performances to help you improve and get better and better."*
>
> **Chris Smalling - Manchester United FC**

Of course, it can be very easy to lose focus and it's unlikely you will go through a full career without losing your focus at some point; you have to ensure you regain that focus as quickly as possible. If you're someone who loses your focus and concentration on a regular basis – are you in danger of appearing like an unreliable player? Are you someone that the manager may be reluctant to turn to - when selecting his team?

> *"The psychological side of the game is massively important. It's of huge benefit to think in a positive manner and good preparation backs up that train of thought.*
>
> *Let's face it, you are never going to be 100% for every game; but instead of being 100% for five out of ten games you can be 100% for eight or nine games with the right preparation. Consequently, because you are safe in the knowledge that you have prepared properly - your mental strength, your confidence, and your ability to handle situations will all improve."*
>
> **Steve Claridge - Former Leicester, Portsmouth, Birmingham & Others**

> *"Losing focus is something you do as a young lad. Then, you find you become more focused as an adult because you know how to deal with it all. It's so important you deal with a loss of focus quickly as, in a sense, you're self-employed. Yes, you have contracts with clubs but they don't have to play you in a certain number of games, or keep you at the club. So you have to look after yourself."*
>
> **Guy Branston (co-author) - a personal reflection**

Everyone has guilty moments (even guilty sessions) throughout their career. You feel guilty about what you've eaten, you feel guilty about staying up late, you feel guilty for not getting enough sleep, and you feel guilty when you're late for training. These scenarios can affect you mentally and lead to a loss of focus.

You've got to get yourself right. You are the one who is ultimately responsible for getting enough food, enough sleep, and enough fluid on-board. You don't want to walk onto the training pitch for a two-to-three hour intensive session (that the normal person and even some other players won't be able to cope with) with doubt hanging over you. This will take focus away from the session you are confronted with.

> *"Sleeping patterns, eating patterns and stuff like that are massively important, and I think it's something that some kids are not given enough advice about.*
>
> *Having the right amount of sleep determines how you feel for the rest of the day, so surely that must be one of the most important things that should be highlighted to kids? But the advice and guidance on sleeping patterns isn't there.*
>
> *I realized very quickly that I needed the right amount of sleep; too much and I'd feel listless, and too little I'd be tired. This is all part and parcel of what you do."*
>
> **Steve Claridge - Former Leicester, Portsmouth, Birmingham & Others**

"The determination, dedication and focus you have to put into football is crazy. Eating the right food, getting the right sleep, watching what you eat during the off-season."

Matt Fish - Gillingham FC

"I've always been quite professional, even when I was youngster. I was careful what I ate and made sure if I had a game the next day I would go to bed early."

Jonathan Meades - Oxford United FC

Becoming and remaining focused can be hard, sometimes, as a youngster - but you've got to do it. There are so many other players within the squad biting at your heels to take your position. During your career there is no point when you have the opportunity to relax and take your foot off the pedal. There will be certain things in life that you cannot control but your focus and how you can be a top *professional* does not fall into that category. Let players looking to take your shirt be aware you are there; show them who's boss, remind them *why* you have the shirt, and make them aware it's going to take a monumental effort to take it from you.

Never underestimate your opposition

Naturally, getting yourself motivated and 'up' for huge clashes, with opposition in and around you in the table, is easy. But where things can prove more difficult is when you are playing so-called 'weaker' opposition.

Chapter 4

> *"The only time I underestimated the opposition was when I had moved club from a higher division to a lower division. I was doing really well in the division higher but I dropped down a league so I could live more locally to my family. It only affected me for a few games, and I found it hard getting focused as I was playing a Conference side that had just been promoted.*
>
> *I had to tell myself: you can't just cruise through this. Who do you think you are? My self-talk before the game, whoever the opposition, is always of high intensity with set targets of what I want to achieve out of the game.*
>
> *When I first started out, if I could see there was an easier team coming up - I found myself a bit more relaxed in the training sessions the week before. In the same way, if it was a top-of-the-table clash my intensity in training would go up. I could see the mood changing with my teammates. I made sure I stamped out these differences in approach early on within my own career. You simply cannot progress that way."*
>
> **Guy Branston (co-author) - a personal reflection**

If you start taking your foot off the pedal someone will catch you out. You've got to make sure you are looking over your shoulder all the time as someone wants your shirt, someone wants to take the ball from you, that extra £500 a week in wages from you, that appearance money, that win bonus. People want to do that. That's just sport. And that is why we love it so much. It's a battle, it's about survival of the fittest; these are the sort of things you want to be involved in.

It is essential you rid yourself of any mindset that you ever play a 'lesser' side. This should not be as hard as it seems; who's to say the opposition are a lesser side anyway? The league table doesn't always show you what is happening within a football club.

Delete your thoughts and perceptions of superiority. Treat and prepare for every game to the best of your abilities. At the end of the day every game is the same: people are always watching you, and always judging you.

External influences should not affect your focus

Footballers are all different and come from various backgrounds and upbringings. There may be things going on at home, or within your family, that are playing on your mind but you must ensure you don't bring them onto the training ground or into a game. When you are in your working environment you should only be concentrating on one thing - and that's football!

As talked about previously, in chapter 2, choosing the right friends that will support you (and not pressure you into picking up bad habits) throughout your footballing journey is integral to keeping focused.

"I had the discipline because I didn't know anything else. I wasn't going out drinking or anything before I went to university. I still look back now and wonder how I disciplined myself but at the time I didn't think anything of it.

I didn't really go out mid-week and obviously at university it's a big part of student life. I had a really good set of friends who were really understanding and just accepted the fact that I played football and didn't go out with them all the time."

Neill Collins - Sheffield United FC

"I didn't really have a problem going out and stuff like that; I was lucky I had decent friends around me."

Ben Amos - Manchester United FC

Focus can often be affected by other people. If you let it! Throughout your career, and across all levels, people will always look to judge you. Certain people are always waiting for you to fail, they can't wait to badmouth you and put you down. A lot of people only go to games to moan and shout, they don't go there to be positive. Ignore it and don't take it personally. Don't let negativity from other people put you off and affect you from performing at the top of your game. Stay focused and let your football do the talking.

Summary

You have to be very strong-minded to stay completely focused for such long periods of time. There will be the occasional weak moment, along the way, when your mind begins to wander, and your challenge is to ensure you get back, and focused, as quickly as possible.

A 90-minute game requires complete concentration throughout; too many lapses in concentration can only have negative effects on your development, and might even have the potential to stifle progress within the game. Get your head right from an early age and carry it, with you, through the entirety of your footballing journey.

Top tips from this chapter:

- If suitable, set yourself challenging goals to help channel your focus to reaching those goals.
- Try to concentrate and remain focused throughout the duration of your footballing life.
- You will probably have weak moments where you lose concentration. When they happen, make sure you get back on track as soon as possible.
- Play every game with top intensity and focus regardless of the opposition.
- Stay on your toes and never become smug with your status in the team. Someone will always be looking to pounce on any opportunity to take your position.
- Channel your focus on football and don't let external influences affect you from reaching your goals.

5

Use Disappointment as Motivation to Achieve

Receiving negative news is not nice for anyone and there aren't too many professional footballers who have made it to where they are today without receiving disappointing news somewhere along the way.

Generally speaking disappointment is part of life, and most of us have received discouraging news at some point. But these disappointments can be used as learning points; individuals can ensure the same thing doesn't happen to them again. Disappointment and failure can actually help drive a person forwards.

Disappointment can be processed in different ways. You can sit there and feel sorry for yourself - dwelling on what might have been - or you can dust yourself down and go again. The way in which disheartening news is dealt with can help determine how likely it is that you'll recognise your full footballing potential, and play at the highest standard possible.

> *"At times it may seem hard to enjoy playing football because, along the way, you will suffer disappointment whether that's not being picked to play one week or not getting through a trial. Both of which I have suffered from a young age. But you have to keep going because when you do succeed it will give you that real satisfaction that we all crave for in life.*
>
> *Like myself, when you do end up getting through your next trial you can know - deep down inside - that the disappointment you suffered earlier made you much stronger for it. It enabled you to succeed later on, when the time was meant to be."*

Chris Smalling - Manchester United FC

Don't let negativity stop you

In football, disappointing news or negative comments can come from a whole host of people including family, friends, coaches and fans. Nonetheless, if your desire and determination is to make it in the game, it's important you use these comments as motivation to prove the people concerned wrong.

> *"I will tell you about the road to success. It's not a straight road, there's a lot of curves (ups and downs), but it's how you react to the down times that defines you. I was last to get offered a scholarship at Crystal Palace and that was hard! If you think that was my hard work finished, you are wrong. To get to pro is ten times harder. I didn't have a successful first year as a scholar, but in my second year I was showing signs of steady improvement, and started enjoying my football again.*
>
> *Yet again, I was last to be offered pro! Out of eight of us, only four were offered a one year pro contract, and I was over the moon. I just kept working hard at my game and, in my spare time, doing as much as I could to gain an advantage. In my eyes it was working. I was the first and only one out of the four to play in the first team. The year after that I was the only one left at Crystal Palace in my age group! Which was an achievement in itself."*

Matt Parsons - Plymouth Argyle FC

The *only* way to deal with negative comments; is to take them on the chin and don't let them drag you down.

Be prepared, for example, to receive comments (potentially) from family encouraging you to pursue a different career path – something where the odds are more stacked in your favour. Not every player is lucky enough to have the full support and backing of their family straightaway. This is not because they don't want you to achieve, and be a success in life, they are just aware of the competitive nature of the industry and appreciate how tough it is to break through and make a living.

"I can recall several times, when asked what I wanted to be when I was older, how the responses were not the most encouraging. Comments like, "But what about a real job" and even sometimes a slight chuckle - until they realised how serious I actually was.

I had asked my parents several times about moving to England to pursue my dream and at the age of 16 I was given an opportunity."

Jonte Smith - Crawley Town FC

Be strong and stand up for yourself

If you are someone that constantly needs to be loved and regularly requires an arm put around your shoulder, you will need to change your ways as football is a selfish sport. It's not the sort of industry where you are constantly praised and have a comforting mentor around you when times are hard. It may happen at academy level when you are a lot younger but as soon as you hit first team professional level football - it all changes. Fellow players are going to take the mick, you become involved in an often ruthless dressing room, things are going to be said that you're going to get upset about. But forget it! Don't take it personally! It happens, and you'll have to learn to deal with it in a *positive manner*. The sooner you do that, the quicker you'll gain the respect of the dressing room and become one of the lads.

> "*I can cope with the dressing room today but there are still some days I don't want to go in the dressing room, some days I just want to sit in my car until training starts. But you can't live like that, you have to stick your chest out and see what bounces off it. You will deal with it! If you're getting it in the ear from your family and your coach - you will be able to cope with it. You have to tell yourself that.*"

Guy Branston (co-author) - a personal reflection

Dust yourself down and prove the doubters wrong

Being told you are not quite good enough, or no longer required at a club, is one of the biggest disappointments faced by players across the country; whether that's at a trial, academy level, or at various stages throughout a professional player's career. The news can be hard to take. This is when you need to be mentally strong. Rather than letting bad news put you off - use it as extra motivation to prove the doubters wrong.

> "*When I was let go by Crewe I think it made me more determined once I got my chance at United. A bit of fate and bit of luck was involved with that, but once I had that chance I had that drive. I mentioned blowing the other keepers out of the water in training. I just wasn't going to let being released happen to me again. I knew that my biggest strength was to push my body to places no one else was prepared to go.*"

Ben Amos - Manchester United FC

"There are many disappointments in football and one of them is being let go, or being told you're being put on the transfer list.

I experienced this at Bolton, after my five year contract had finished, I was told by Owen Coyle that he wasn't going to offer me another contract. I was devastated when I got told and didn't know what to do, I remember walking out of his office and thinking 'I'm going to prove you wrong'. What he said to me spurred me on to make it as a footballer."

Chris Stokes - Forest Green Rovers FC

"At the time, Cardiff City was a Championship club and Dave Jones was the manager. He was quite honest with me and he just said, "I don't think you're a Championship footballer." He added, "I believe you'll have a career in football but it's not going to happen for you at Cardiff City."

Obviously if you are let go from a football club you want to go and prove someone wrong, you want to prove you're good enough, so I had that drive anyway."

Dan Parslow - York City FC

"I signed for Millwall on a short-term contract and I then went to Stevenage under Peter Taylor. Peter Taylor left and the new manager came in and straightaway put me on the transfer list; to be that fresh into football and get put on the transfer list - not knowing what to do and where to go - I was sort of lost really.

The only thing I could do was to work as hard as I possibly could to impress, and I ended up staying at Stevenage under the same manager for two and a half years.

To date that was probably the toughest obstacle I've had to overcome."

Peter Vincenti - Rochdale AFC

"There is always someone that's going to say you're not good enough to make it, and it's not the end of the world.

When Alex Ferguson released me, he assured me that I would have a career in the game, but nothing is set in stone and you can never be sure.

That gave me the determination to leave home and take an opportunity to pursue a career in football."

Mike Pollitt - Wigan Athletic FC

"I think the criticism I received regarding my physicality was the best thing that happened to me, to be honest, as it made me more determined to prove people wrong. A lot of professional sports people who are a lot more successful than me have this thing about proving people wrong.

I think playing over 100 league games before I went to Sunderland helped me develop a lot more. I think, for example, that when I went down to Sunderland - in comparison to a lot of players in the academy system - I was probably ahead of them, whereas two years before, they were probably ahead of me. I think this was because I was playing games and you learn so much more playing in games than you do training in an academy. I think that's probably why clubs loaning out young players has become so important these days."

Neill Collins - Sheffield United FC

"Other than the challenges of trying to stay in the team, and at a club in administration, my next test came when Gary Mills made it clear my time at Notts County was up, and I was sent to Scarborough on loan. It went well and, despite being released by Notts, the Scarborough manager, Russell Slade, had just moved to Grimsby in League Two and told me to come and sign in pre-season.

When I got there, however, I was told it was a trial and after two weeks of pre-season he said no, and I was left club-less with the season a week or two from starting. I called Scarborough whose left back had been sent off in pre-season and they asked me to come and help them out - but with no promise of a contract.

I played the first game and they came to me with an offer. It was about 70% less than what I was on at Notts County but with no options and a burning desire to prove myself as a footballer I said yes and played the next two seasons on 10 month contracts while losing money every month!"

Kevin Nicholson - Torquay United FC

"My biggest regret was leaving Leicester. That was nearly 15 years ago and I'm still in the game. I was so upset about leaving my local side, and leaving a massive club. You've just got to keep your head up, and get on with these things, and take opportunities as they arise."

Guy Branston (co-author) - a personal reflection

Sorry you're not selected today

A very demoralizing and more regular disappointment for a number of players is hearing the team selection being announced, and your name is not included. Sometimes you are not even in the squad.

Chapter 5

"If you want to sit on the bench every week and watch someone else be a success then good for you, but I didn't want that so I left Leicester. I didn't want a career where I was sitting on the bench and watching people progress in front of me, I wanted to be the one progressing.

These disappointments added to my determination and aggression to succeed. Aggression can be a positive thing. It can also be a hindrance, so you have to turn aggression into a positive thing, standing up for yourself, being aggressive to win the ball back, being able to cope with situations when people are getting on at you."

Guy Branston (co-author) - a personal reflection

It's important you don't take non-inclusion in a manager's team selection personally, as there can be many reasons for it. For example, he may feel you need a rest as he doesn't want to burn you out, or you could be a technically gifted ball player and your team may be coming up against a big, strong team that battle hard and play the long ball. In other words, the particular game may not suit you. Or your non-selection could simply be because you had an 'off' game the previous week. Every player, even at the very highest level, has off days, so remain positive.

The overall situation should be clear in your mind, and you should understand why the manager is getting on at you, and why he isn't selecting you.

"There was a spell this season when we weren't winning. We were conceding goals and I got dropped. Did I deserve to get dropped? No, I didn't. But the manager chose me and made me the scapegoat. But I didn't mind because I understand where he was coming from with it.

I understand the game that I play in and the manager is the man picking the side. You have to respect that. He's your boss who brings you to the football club to do well for him, the last thing he wants you to do is fail. So, don't take being dropped too personally. Accept his decision, take it on-board, and train hard so you are prepared for the time when an opportunity arises again to win your place back.

I know I make it sound simple but it can literally be that simple."

Guy Branston (co-author) - a personal reflection

Summary

You should always aim high. But, in doing so, do not become disappointed at the first thing that goes wrong in your career. If you're going to be disappointed at the first thing that goes wrong - you shouldn't be playing football. Get your head around the fact that there are going to be stacks of things that go wrong, every day.

The Manager won't speak to you at training, that's not the end of your career. You're not going to get picked for the team for a few weeks, that's not the end of your career.

There will be times when you are going to come home frustrated that you haven't had enough of an integral role in training. There *will be* lots of disappointments at all stages of your career. The best players bounce back from these moments.

Football is an industry of hard graft. If you want to be a professional footballer, you don't just 'have' this fabulous lifestyle, you have to put lots 'in' to get to that point. And the lower down you play the harder it is.

If you're reading this book and have been rejected at academy level, or even at an early stage as a professional footballer, but want to kick on again because you are still young enough, use this book as a positive. Use the real life examples of the pro players above who have had their downs and low points. If they can come out

Chapter 5

the other side and flourish following disappointment - why can't you?

Top tips from this chapter:

- Various people will say things you don't want to hear. Don't take their comments to heart. If you want something bad enough - go ahead and try to get it.
- Dressing rooms can be a daunting place especially for new players. Take the banter with a pinch of salt, integrate with the lads, and you will gain the respect of the dressing room in no time.
- Don't take negative comments personally or let them get you down for too long. Use the comments to fuel extra desire and provide an additional driving force to succeed.
- There are plenty of football clubs around, so if you're not wanted at one take an opportunity at another.
- Things will go wrong on the road to sustaining a life as a professional footballer. There *will be* a lot of ups and downs, just go out there and give it your best shot.
- Disappointment will have been endured by almost every professional footballer at some point. Follow their examples and use disappointment as your motivation to flourish and prove people wrong.

6

Setbacks are Part of the Game

Setbacks are a big part of football. They can be demoralizing, frustrating, and can leave you with pessimistic thoughts as to whether (or not) you'll come out the other side and carry on living your dream. The way players come back stronger, and continue to progress from these setbacks is commendable, and requires a great deal of determination and positive thinking.

Sorry, you're no longer part of the club's plans

Unfortunately, a large number of young hopefuls, up and down the country, are released or rejected by clubs every season.

Rejection by a club is one of the hardest setbacks to take, especially at a young age. A rejection often leaves people wondering whether they are, in fact, good enough to pursue the footballing dream.

Chapter 6

"Like a lot of footballers, making it as a pro didn't come without setbacks. Being released from Crewe was the first real setback that sticks in my mind. Obviously it was a shock, and at a young age as well - when you're hoping to make it. I'd just got my foot on the ladder and then it was taken away from me. That was my biggest setback."

Ben Amos - Manchester United FC

"I think it's a test of character when you get knocks in football. I was told, at 20, that I wasn't wanted at Cardiff along with a few others that were released the same day; my attitude was I'm willing to go wherever, whenever, to have a chance of playing football.

There were some that didn't want to move away from home, they were quite happy to be around people they loved and they weren't willing to go that extra yard and give it a shot. They were quite happy to drop out of football and do something else. Not necessarily drop out of football altogether but not play professionally, and just pick up a few quid a week playing part-time football, so they could still be at home."

Dan Parslow - York City FC

"There have been quite a few setbacks I've faced. I left Manchester United when I was a 19 year old. You get told by Alex Ferguson you are not going to be at the club anymore and I was left asking myself what am I going to do now?

Bury gave me a chance to go there on trial and I dropped down the leagues to give myself a chance of staying in the game. I didn't play in the first team at Bury, I was playing for the reserves and couldn't see myself getting into the first team. So, I then went to Lincoln and that's where I made my professional debut. I felt I needed to get some games as I was approaching 20 and I still hadn't played a league game.

So I left home and moved to Lincoln to get those games playing league football under my belt."

Mike Pollitt - Wigan Athletic FC

"A lot of footballers have to deal with setbacks at some stage and, at the age of 18 when I had reached the end of my two year scholarship, I was released by Crystal Palace. After being head boy and captain in my final year I thought I was in a good position to receive a pro contract. Unfortunately I didn't and, as it turned out, it was a blessing in disguise. At the time, though, I didn't know what I was going to do.

When all you have done is football, football, football, to then be told you are being let go is the worst feeling in the world. Only the lads that are determined and mentally strong have gone on to make it as pros from my age group."

Matt Fish - Gillingham FC

"At 16, I went on trial with local football league side Dagenham and Redbridge where I was knocked back and basically told that I wasn't good enough for their academy side. This was hard to take as I thought this would have been one of my last chances to get a shot at being a professional."

Jack Baldwin - Peterborough United FC

"When I was younger I couldn't get into the County team and that was quite hard to take. Obviously, rejection for anything is hard and County was the best level at that time, and I didn't make it, which was really tough to take, but these things happen in football.

It was a case of dusting myself down and having my family around me who were always pushing me and giving me the confidence to carry on.

Also, at St Albans when I made it into the first team, I had been there a year or so and they said I wasn't good enough.

It was a case of either staying there and just sitting on the bench or dropping another division. That was a very big decision as I had been through the youth system and made it into the first team and I thought it was going to be an upwards spiral from there; but it went the opposite direction.

Again that was really disappointing and I think that took me maybe half a season when I was at Arseley Town to accept that it wasn't going to change. I had to just get my head down and work hard and from that I moved to Dagenham, which was great.

With rejection - you've just got to kind of accept it, accept what they have said, and have that confidence and belief in your own ability; it doesn't matter what anyone says, you are going to achieve what you want to achieve."

Craig Mackail-Smith - Brighton & Hove Albion FC

Being released or told you are surplus to requirements at your current club continues throughout the footballing journey. It's key to treat a move to a new club as an exciting time rather than dwell on the disappointment of being released. Look for opportunities and grasp them with both hands as they present themselves. The unknowns of a club move can be a really exciting change to your life.

You'll be side-lined for a while

There is never a good time to get injured but there's a strong possibility it will happen at some stage given the intense, physically demanding, competitive contact sport you are involved in.

Recovering and enduring a long course of rehabilitation can be painstaking and hugely frustrating - especially when you see the rest of the team training and playing matches. It's important you take note of encouraging improvements and look towards the light at the end of the tunnel.

"In the first year of my professional contract, I went to Norway and when I came back I was doing really well and I was looking forward to making my debut. There was even talk of me, maybe, getting a starting place in the FA Cup team but unfortunately my knee gave way, and I had something called patella tendonitis which quite a lot of footballers have. That kept me out for about nine months. I ended up having an operation on my knee, so that was a bit of a nightmare.

About a month after coming back from my knee problems I broke my nose playing for Wales, which I had another operation to sort out. And then I came back from that and had something called compartment syndrome in my calves, which I had another operation for and that kept me out for another six months.

So, the first two years of my professional career at Cardiff were plagued with injuries, which I couldn't really do much about."

Jonathan Meades - Oxford United FC

"During my second season as a pro at Hartlepool I was enjoying a good run of form in the first team when I suffered a knee injury that put me out for 3/4 weeks. Initially I was preparing for six weeks on the sideline which would have meant I wouldn't have played again that season, as the injury occurred towards the back end of the campaign. However, I stuck to my strict rehab programme, and worked hard at it, and I was back for the final three or four games of the season."

Jack Baldwin - Peterborough United FC

"A big thing in football that every footballer hates is being injured. I have had one major injury in my career so far and these setbacks are hard to deal with when you can't play and have to spend hours and hours in the gym trying to get fit!

I ruptured my anterior cruciate ligament at 14 in my first game for Bolton; I was devastated when I found out that I couldn't play for 12 months. I was fortunate to have great physios who helped me recover but it was hard to stay positive and not get down. There were times when I got really down, and depressed, and it was tough watching your team mates play when you were not able to.

I managed to get through this and definitely learned that being injured is part and parcel of football and you need to stay strong, think positively, and remember the harder you work at getting back to fitness - the quicker you're back playing."

Chris Stokes - Forest Green Rovers FC

"I've had an Achilles injury that has kept me out for a year, so this season has been my toughest because I've never missed this amount of time in football before. Watching from the side-lines, week-in week-out, for a year has been hard. It's been mentally draining to see the boys train and play and not be able to physically do it.

I think it's been a good test of character; it's given me more of a drive now and more of an appreciation of what I've got, and what can be taken away by a training injury or an injury in a game.

With injuries I think you have to believe in yourself and believe you are going to get through it. Take everyday as it comes, enjoy everyday and see it as a kind of stepping-stone to getting fit."

Craig Mackail-Smith - Brighton & Hove Albion FC

"I'm someone that, if faced with a setback, it makes me more determined. Blimey I've had enough of them.

I didn't even finish my apprenticeship at Portsmouth; I partly had myself to blame and also the fella who took us wasn't giving us a level playing field.

The first game after I was told I wasn't good enough for Portsmouth I actually played a game at Fratton Park for the County side and broke my ankle badly in two places; so, as you can imagine, it was a bit of a double whammy. I'd been thrown out of Pompey and I'd also broken my ankle.

I was out for the best part of eight months and I think that is when you realize: this is it, you're either going to take this seriously and do it properly, or you are going to fall by the wayside.

So I started to really get my head down, I had to do three jobs just so I could survive and get me some time to do what I wanted to do. Obviously they couldn't be jobs I wasn't able to leave so I was doing a bit of market gardening. I had a little stall and I also did some landscaping; and that sort of tided me over until I managed to get back into the game. It also very quickly made me realize, even with the obvious disappointments that lay ahead, football was still a) what I wanted to do and b) a fantastic life to lead.

That was a setback, and I've had one or two things that have happened to me as a manager that, at times, have been staggeringly unfair, but there you go. I'm afraid that's just football!"

Steve Claridge - Former Leicester, Portsmouth, Birmingham & Others

Unfortunately some players receive injuries they cannot recover from, which subsequently cuts short their careers. It's not nice to think about this but it's something that must be considered, as the reality is it can happen. It's a terrible shame when dreams are shattered and the predicament can be very hard to take; however you need to try and get yourself into a mindset that life does go on, and there is a life after football.

"My career finished at 25 through injury. I've had 18 operations and 13 of them were on my knees. I never had trouble through my teen years with any type of injuries, then I had a minor operation on my knee cartilage at Leicester, then I got a bad tackle about eight months into my contract at Sunderland and from then on that knee kept going.

So at 24 years old I went to see the most renowned surgeon in the world for sports injuries and he went in, had a look, and came back out and said to me, "I don't think you should ever play professional sport again." He continued, "Three or four more injuries on your knees and it will just be bone on bone and you'll have arthritis before you're 30 and you don't want to go down that road."

I was talking to a lad who was at Leicester academy and he had a knee injury and had to quit football, and I said to him I feel sorry for you as you never even reached your dreams and he said, "I feel sorry for you more, as you made your dream, you got there and then it was taken away from you. I don't know what it's like to be a pro footballer, so it's not as bad for me." And that's how he saw the situation. And when I thought about it, I thought he was probably right as he didn't taste the highs of playing in front of 60-70 thousand people some weeks."

Matt Piper - Former Leicester City FC & Sunderland AFC

Stuck in the mud

Every player likes to see improvement and progression in their game especially when they have been working hard at various aspects in the hope of improving themselves.

When you are getting your head down and working yourself into the ground and you are not progressing or moving forward – things can seem very discouraging. It may seem as though - no matter what you do - you appear to remain at the same level. You may even see this as a major setback in your development.

Try not to worry. Generally, when you work at something tirelessly, the rewards will eventually come. Remember the old cliché - 'practice makes perfect'. There can be many contributing factors that must work in sync so you are in the best possible physical and mental state to train at the right intensity to progress. Anything from a minor injury to trouble sleeping can inhibit your ability to work at your maximum level.

Progression can happen over so many different timeframes you may find, at some stages of your career, that you see improvements over a few weeks, other times months, and sometimes even years.

Progress won't happen overnight - so keep working hard. In fact, it may sometimes not be hugely noticeable what benefit that hard work is having but be reassured that even remaining at your current level is hugely important and a reluctance to maintain your work rate can see a rapid decline in your performances. In fact, you usually lose the benefits you have gained from the good work you've been doing quicker than you see the benefits of the hard work you've put in. So, make sure you are, at the very least, keeping up the same intensity.

Prolonged dip in form

If you experience a prolonged dip in form, don't worry. Every player, even the top performing players in world football, suffers dips in form. For example, a striker may have a hot streak where whatever he touches (regardless of the angle or distance) hits the back of the net. Then, the same player - six weeks later - 'couldn't hit a barn door' and may not score for 10 games.

Ride these tough patches and don't let them dent your confidence too much. You will have bad training sessions and poor performances in matches from time to time but as long as you're working your socks off, you will still be a valuable member of the team and your form will (over time) return. It may take a lot longer than anticipated but keep the faith and continue to try and enjoy your football.

> *"I've had dips in form numerous times. I've gone through dips in form when I haven't been happy with myself. I have moved to a new club with a fantastic opportunity and it hasn't worked out for me on the pitch.*
>
> *You will come out the other side, there is no doubt about it. If you work hard you'll come out the other side. There is no point beating yourself up about it. Don't get me wrong, it's very hard at the time but it's not going to last long. You will get your confidence back."*
>
> **Guy Branston (co-author) - a personal reflection**

> *"Setbacks also include smaller things like poor training sessions that affect you mentally, which sometimes left me doubting my own ability. But you just have to stay strong and have the mental toughness to pull you through any situation. Being a professional footballer is, for the majority of the time, about being mentally strong more than anything."*
>
> **Jack Baldwin - Peterborough United FC**

> *"You will have bad games that you have to learn to recover from. That is a skill in itself, but class is permanent after all."*
>
> **Ben Amos - Manchester United FC**

The reason why players continue to be selected by managers when suffering a dip in form is that they continue to perform well in training and they still work hard in matches. Football fans only see a dip in form on a Saturday afternoon; they don't see how a player is performing during training throughout the week. If a player isn't performing to a high standard in training, and matches, the manager won't pick them. It's as simple as that. A manager standing by a player going through a tough time on the pitch gives the player a huge boost as it shows the manager still has faith in them.

The problem arises when a dip in form leads to your manager taking you out of the firing line and resting you from the team. Sometimes you then try too hard to get back to your best and it can make things worse. The best way to rediscover form is to continue playing the *way you have always played*, and gain as much match practice as possible. Let's face it - how else can you recapture your top form? In addition to sitting on the bench for a number of weeks, it could be a good idea when the first team does not have a fixture to ask the manager to allow you to have a few run outs for the reserves at a lower level, to help you regain your confidence.

A new manager usually brings a new style of play

Football is a results-based business and, sadly, if results take a turn for the worse managers aren't always given much time to fix matters. Consequently, and we see this a lot at professional club level, a new manager is put in place.

"It happens all the time, a new manager comes in and changes the structure and makes changes to the squad. It's something I have never been able to get my head around. I feel it's an area football clubs need to address. If a new manager, on arrival, signs one or two players it is understandable, but some managers bring in whole new squads which is ridiculous and I don't understand how the club's infrastructure can handle it."

Guy Branston (co-author) - a personal reflection

When a new manager comes in, various issues arise. These include what happens to the youth team, and what happens to the players coming through. A change of manager often makes it difficult to give the club an identity in terms of the style of football they play, and the filter down through to the coaches of the youth age groups can get messy. Ultimately, youth coaches are there to develop players that, over time, will progress into the first team of a football club.

A new manager can have huge effects on all the playing staff within a club; a change provides a clean slate and a chance for fringe players to stake their claims. It can make regular starters feel a bit nervous as they feel their starting positions could be under threat. The previous manager may have brought you into the club but as soon as a new manager is appointed you are no longer sure if you will be his first choice.

> *"I've seen it and been through it so many times that it's water off a duck's back. If the manager doesn't want me I will move on. If the manager does want me then I will stay there. It's something you have to expect to deal with as footballers. A change of management is part of the job."*
>
> **Guy Branston (co-author) - a personal reflection**

> *"Dave Jones got sacked as manager and was replaced by Malky Mackay and he didn't really get a chance to see me play, to be fair. I had a couple of reserve games when he came in, then I was injured for a lot of the time, and eventually got released.*
>
> *I then went on trial for Bournemouth and did well there and got signed for two years. A similar kind of thing happened there, I was in and around the first team and the manager at the time got fired. Another manager came in and I wasn't in contention."*
>
> **Jonathan Meades - Oxford United FC**

> *"My first setback was when Paul Jewell took over at Sheffield Wednesday and took a dislike to me. I realised my time was up as I had never played in the Premier League. Ironically he gave me my one appearance in the Championship before I left."*
>
> **Kevin Nicholson - Torquay United FC**

Being flexible, attentive, and having a willingness to learn and adapt to a new manager's philosophy towards the game will aid you in continuing a career at a specific club. Alternatively if you do begin to realise, after giving it your all, that you simply don't fit into the new manager's plan, don't panic! There are plenty of other teams around and sometimes it's a case of 'as one door shuts another door opens'.

Summary

Setbacks form part of many professional footballers' histories. They can really leave you feeling down. The reason why professional sportsmen and women continue to thrive is because they get up and go again. Follow their examples and do the same; keep positive, stay optimistic and come back stronger.

Top tips from this chapter:

- A club letting you go isn't nice, but pick yourself up and find yourself another club.
- Injuries can lead to a long road to recovery. Take positives when there are improvements in your condition and remember that many players have suffered similar injuries and come out the other side.
- Progression takes time but if you apply yourself - you will eventually see the results.
- Every player has dips in form. Don't panic. A dip in form will come to an end.
- If a new manager comes in, embrace his training methods and tactical style of play, and fully commit to his running of the team. If he still won't play you, move to a club that will.

7

Football is Based on a Lot of Opinions

Football, like many things in life, is based on opinions. And these opinions will exist right the way through your career. Parents, friends, family, fans, managers, coaches and team mates will all have an opinion on your footballing ability - good or bad.

It's difficult to be every club's cup of tea

The first meaningful opinions that can initially open (or close) doors for you are from coaches, managers, and the scouts that represent a club.

Chapter 7

If you are presented with a trial, or are nearing a time when a club has to judge whether (or not) they think you can step up to the first team at a professional level, decisions will be made. The impact of these decisions can leave you feeling hugely joyful or upset and down in the dumps.

If it's a negative outcome, ask yourself 'so what'? If a decision is made not to take up your services (a certain manager or club may not want you, for example) - that's not to say every club will think the same way. The great thing about the English game is that there are a large number of opportunities to participate with football clubs at a variety of different levels. In other words, there is nearly always the prospect to play somewhere else if one club doesn't select you to progress through their ranks.

> *"Football is based a lot on opinions. I've seen it where one person's opinion is so different to another's. For instance if you're at a club, and you don't quite make it, get released, or there's one coach that doesn't think you're good enough, that definitely doesn't mean you're not going to make it.*
>
> *Just keep your head up, keep trying and give it your best, because there are so many different opinions of players in football, and one coach's opinion doesn't count for every coach. So if things don't work out straightaway, that doesn't mean it's over."*
>
> **Jonathan Meades - Oxford United FC**

By all means aim to play at the highest level you can, but don't let the first rejection at a certain level stop you from trying your luck at a different club. Regular playing time is what you should strive for.

"I was offered schoolboy/YTS/Pro contracts at Arsenal, Manchester City, Derby and Sheffield Wednesday. I chose Sheffield Wednesday as I got on very well with the scout, a great man called Ernie Stevens, and the head of youth there, the late Clive Baker. Along with the setup, I thought that a middle-of-the-road Premier League team would give me the best chance to play first team football the quickest. In retrospect I should have signed for Arsenal as they had the best infrastructure, coaching, and a proven record with young players.

I would recommend any young player to start as high as they can!"

Kevin Nicholson - Torquay United FC

There can also be an element of luck involved.

"I do think you need luck, there's no hiding away from that. For instance, if you go on a trial and don't get through, it's one person's opinion of you and if someone else was watching you that day, they may have fancied you and put you through. That is football, it's all about opinions so it's tough and you do need that luck."

Dan Parslow - York City FC

"Sometimes you need a bit of luck as you can make the wrong decision. Before signing for Lincoln, I nearly went out of the professional game altogether and signed for Altrincham who were in the Conference at the time. My Dad wouldn't let me go there and fortunately I didn't as I then received the chance to go to Lincoln who were playing League football.

They say that when you come out of the professional game it's very hard to get back in, so that was something I took on-board and luckily I listened. Sometimes you do need that luck of being in the right place at the right time and I do believe luck plays a part."

Mike Pollitt - Wigan Athletic FC

Luck, however, is not necessarily some mystical, or magical, thing. There is a famous quote from the golfer Gary Player. He said: "The more I practise, the luckier I get." Wise words!

If you are continually being knocked back, or are consistently not being selected, drop down a level or two; there is no shame in that. Playing regular football is vitally important for your own personal progression and the only way you will fully enjoy the game is to be fully *involved* within the game. And that stems from regular game time.

> *"I had a tough time trying to find another club after I was released from Bolton Wanderers, as there were hundreds of other people just like me who were out of contract trying to find another club. I had trials at Crewe, Walsall, Doncaster, Bury, and Morecombe but none of them worked out for different reasons, and come September I was still without a club.*
>
> *This was hard to deal with as this was the first time in my life that I thought I'm not going to be able to play football for a living anymore and I'm going to have to find myself a job. I had a talk with my family and I decided to give it two more months and if I couldn't find a club then that would be it. This was a huge eye opener for me and being in that situation made me want to be a footballer even more than I did before. I got a call from the manager of Forest Green to come play a game so he could watch me play and the rest is history.*
>
> *I've been at Forest Green for three seasons now. I'm playing regularly, and I'm enjoying being a footballer again."*
>
> **Chris Stokes - Forest Green Rovers FC**

It's not only the clubs and managers that will have their say

With so many people involved in the sport, in different capacities, you will probably experience a large number of conflicting opinions regarding your ability as a footballer. These opinions can come from a vast array of different people.

The Fans and supporters of your team

At the early stages of your career your 'fans' will be limited to your family and friends. However, as you develop and start playing for the reserve team and first team, the number of fans will dramatically increase.

There are a number of fans who love to voice their opinions and have their say, acting as though they know everything about the game. The reality is that 99% of them have never played the game at a professional level (and some may have never even played the game at all) so there will be some individuals who really don't know what they are talking about.

Remember, though, everyone is entitled to their opinion. They have chosen to spend their time and money to come and watch you and your team. However, what you don't have to do is listen to, or take any notice of, their opinions.

"When I signed a two-year pro contract at Gillingham, from non-League Dover, straightaway the fans at Gillingham were unsure about me because of where I had come from.

I did get bad comments from fans and unfortunately for my family they heard some of these comments like "Fish, he's not good enough", "Sub him he's useless". These comments have caused my Mum to only come to the big games at home where she can sit with the families of others players. These types of comments do hurt but they make you stronger and I've ended up turning the fans around to loving me. But, at the time, it's tough to take."

Matt Fish - Gillingham FC

It seems obvious but the general trend is - the better you perform on the pitch the more people will have good things to say about you; if you're playing poorly you'll have more people saying negative things about you. That's just how football is.

> *"All that most fans want is for you to work hard, give it your all, and make sure you are proud to wear the shirt of the club they are supporting."*
>
> **Steve Claridge - Former Leicester, Portsmouth, Birmingham & Others**

Family and Close Friends

Generally speaking (if you are fortunate) family members and close friends want what's best for you and offer you great support and comforting words.

Problems can arise, however, when their praise is 'over the top' and possibly inaccurate. It's perfectly normal for parents, and other close family and friends, to have high opinions of you but in some cases the praise can pull the wool over your eyes. For example, if your parents or close friends constantly tell you you're a great player and enthusiastically tell you how brilliantly you've played every game, you can enter a wonderland and truly believe you're a fabulous player that can take on the world when it may not be the case. You may even stop training as hard as you can, or pushing yourself forwards – you think you have made it!

It's important to remain grounded and not get carried away by the constant praise friends and family give you. It's great they are supportive but evaluate how relevant their opinions are, in the sense of footballing experience and knowledge within the game. The exact same evaluation should be made of parents and friends who are too harsh on you.

If an opinion comes from a former/current professional player or manager it's usually more relevant and trustworthy than from someone outside the game. It's not always the case, of course, as opinions still vary amongst the many professional players and managers. But, generally, they will have a better understanding and perspective as they have experienced what it takes.

> *"I have a close friend back at home who I went to school and sixth form with, and he is a very talented footballer. However, due to various circumstances, injury being the main culprit, he did not sign anywhere as a professional. He was on trial at different clubs at a young age, including Tottenham, QPR, Southend, Stevenage and even travelled to Germany for a trial at a German League side. But, like I said, he was knocked back at all of these clubs because of different reasons, and he is now playing semi-professional football and studying at university. In my opinion, he has the ability to be a professional football player."*
>
> **Jack Baldwin - Peterborough United FC**

Team Mates

Once you have successfully integrated yourself within a club, teammates will hold opinions on your footballing ability. They may even think you're a bad player and avoid passing you the ball.

Alternatively you could be the one worrying about another player's performances and this can distract your attention, and affect your own game, as you are too busy worrying about someone else's game. Make sure you worry about your own performance and not your teammates, or you could find your own standards will begin to slip.

You're going to get players who won't rate you, and who might badmouth you. You will find yourself in a competitive environment every day and players will say things out of jealousy and spite. It shouldn't faze you. The only opinion that counts is that of your manager who selects the team and as long as you continue to play, who cares what your teammates think about you? Remain professional even if teammates are not being professional. Do not let any needle, from a so-called colleague, lead to you becoming hostile or disruptive. Rise above it, and let your football do the talking.

You need to be mentally tough

Negative comments aimed at you will always be part of football, as you simply won't please everyone. It can be difficult to take these comments, especially at the beginning of your career, which is why mental strength is such an important aspect of the modern game. Negativity is something that, at most levels, you don't receive direct help in dealing with. The process of dealing with negative comments is a test of character and in a lot of cases you'll find experience can really help you.

"We've had no help dealing with criticism, whatsoever, at the level I play at. With my time at York City we've had no sports psychologists at all. We've all had to basically just 'deal with it' and everyone's different. It can affect people in different ways. It's not nice to hear criticism, but it's part of football and sport in general and it's how you react to that; some crumble, some rise to it, and some can just block it out so it doesn't affect them whatsoever.

I think the higher you go, the better access you have to these psychologists, because at the end of the day it's all about money. York City, in my time, have been in the Conference for a long time and I think the manager would probably think 'for the cost of sport psychologists I could probably go and get another player in'. Whereas, if you're talking Premier League, where money isn't as much of a problem, they will probably have access to all that. Personally I've been fascinated with the psychological side of the game from my university course. So I've been able to deal with it and rise to the challenge as such.

If you're a player that goes into his shell and this happens regularly, you're likely to find yourself on the sideline and then possibly out of the team altogether. There's a knock-on effect where you could possibly end up out of the game."

Dan Parslow - York City FC

"Mental strength is very important; learning to recover from bad games and dealing with criticism is vital. I did get help with that from a man, not related to the club, called Keith Mincher. He uses something called NLP (Neuro Linguistic Programming), which is basically your self-talk. The things you say to yourself, your sub-conscious will pick up on.

It's basically about having a self-awareness of what you're saying to yourself because a lot of the things you think, you're not aware of - and that's what triggers emotional states you can't control. You can't control what you're not aware of! Things like your breathing and the tone of your self-talk have an effect, so it goes into quite a lot of detail.

I went to see him when I was around 15 or 16 and I've seen him many times since, so that helped me a great deal."

Ben Amos - Manchester United FC

"I think it's so important to be mentally strong. The lows in the game last a lot longer than the highs. The highs, as great as they are, are very short lived.

This is where it's important to educate young lads in the game. I had to pick it up at a later stage as I came in at 21 and there were times when things were being said. You had a bad training session and the manager would be on at you and it affects you. Everyone is human and you can be the most experienced pro in the world but if you hear something that touches a nerve it will affect you. I do, however, feel the longer you are in the game the better you learn to deal with it.

When I first started out heckling from the crowd was really easy to hear. But it's amazing what experience does and now, in a game, when you do something wrong and you know you are going to be heckled, you learn to block it out and go again."

Peter Vincenti - Rochdale AFC

> *"Criticism is hard to deal with and this is where mental strength is so important. I think it's something that comes with experience. Especially me being a goalkeeper in the lower leagues at the beginning of my career. You can hear everything behind your goal at some of the grounds, but you have to try and create a mental block and block all that out. It can be difficult, sometimes, to do that for 90 minutes.*
>
> *I've played in every single league from League Two right the way up to the Premier League and, strangely enough, I find it easier playing in front of bigger crowds than in front of smaller crowds. Maybe that's because you can't hear anything specific because there are so many people there."*
>
> **Mike Pollitt - Wigan Athletic FC**

> *"In this industry you have to be mentally strong. If you're not, you can easily be affected by negativity as there is a lot of it. One poor game and one mistake, and that could be it! You could be at the wrong end of some harsh words from people. But, when things are going well, I believe it's the best feeling you can have!*
>
> *Nothing beats playing well, coming off the pitch with three points and seeing the smiles on your teammates' faces."*
>
> **Matt Parsons - Plymouth Argyle FC**

"If you think everything is going to go swimmingly for you in football, then you're sadly mistaken. I think when you come out of the lows it makes you stronger the next time you go through them, so people either go into a low and cope and come out strong, or they go into a low and they can't come out of it because their character and will to succeed are not strong enough.

You can worry yourself out of a game, you can think you're not as good a player as you might be. You can question your ability to do the job at the level you are playing at.

If you play upfront, and I played upfront for 30 years, people will question you every day, every week and at every game as to whether you are good enough to play there and whether you are able to score enough goals. I was constantly under that spotlight.

I think what you can do is give yourself the best possible opportunity to perform; and you can do this by preparing properly, eating right and sleeping right, both of which are massive.

I always took the view that if I had prepared right during the week I was in a better position to perform at the weekend. Some people think negatively, you know: "We've been on our legs all day", "I'm tired" and "We've worked too hard". I always looked at it in a positive sense; the fitter I was, the further I could run, and the more questions I will ask of the opposition.

At every corner, mentally you will be questioned. People will always judge you and point out your weaknesses and that's something you have to live with.

What you must do is be secure in the knowledge that you are as fit, as strong and as well prepared as you can be, and if you have done that you should have a positive mental state anyway. You have done all you can do and you can't do anymore."

Steve Claridge - Former Leicester, Portsmouth, Birmingham & Others

Chapter 7

Summary

Many people are involved in the game of football – both directly and indirectly. There will, naturally, be a number of individuals who have their say on whether they think you are a good player. It's important you filter through the variety of opinions and take note of the ones that really matter from the important people whose footballing opinion you respect. These are the people who can help you develop and kick on to becoming the best you can be. Take no notice of the opinions that provide no help, or which stem from jealousy, or just people being mean. Take, with a pinch of salt, both positive and negative feedback from people who are in no position to be giving you footballing feedback.

> *"Opinions don't count if you are proving people wrong all the time, and I have done that a lot throughout my career. A lot of people wrote me off and I thrived on that.*
>
> *Even as a 14/15 year old I knew people didn't like me as a footballer but I didn't care. I trusted the opinions of people who had previously played against Real Madrid and I trusted people who had experienced successful careers at Derby and Leicester; I knew they were fantastic coaches. I trusted their opinions and the worth they saw in me as a player over idiots in the street, or my stepdad who had never kicked a ball in his life."*
>
> **Guy Branston (co-author) - a personal reflection**

Top tips from this Chapter:

- One club may not rate you as a player but another club might.
- 'If at first you don't succeed try, try again'.
- Your close friends and family's support shouldn't let you get ahead of yourself.
- Take those opinions that count from reliable sources, and use them to drive forward; the rest you can forget.
- Mental strength is a big part of the game and learning how to deal with (and process) criticism in a positive way will really help you move forward in the game.

8

The Importance of Education

Education and learning are an important and constant part to everyone's life, whether you are a sportsman, a businessman, a chef, a mechanic, or anything else – there is always a need to learn and evolve.

Some people may not see themselves as academic nor enjoy the formal compulsory education system. To be honest, it is unlikely too many people can honestly say they enjoyed, and were passionate about, every single aspect of their time at school.

Unfortunately, with football, you can never be sure if firstly, you will even make it into the professional game and secondly, whether you will stay in the game after receiving your first professional contract. Something as simple as a mistimed tackle could end your career in an instant.

Good basic qualifications in the fundamental subjects can prove very useful in later life and provide you with a great safety net should your career not pan out exactly as you imagined.

It can be hard not to let the bright lights of potential football stardom affect your school focus

Many young hopefuls who have made it into an academy, at a very young age, will have 'bought into' the constant praise they initially receive and maybe get a bit carried away. It's only natural, at such a young age, to believe you are destined to reach the top. It's easy to get caught in the footballing bubble.

"I think some people have the mindset that "I'm going to be a footballer, I don't need anything else, I'm going to achieve it" and sometimes it doesn't work out that way. My parents were really good to me and advised me to push on and make sure I had qualifications, as there is a chance that you won't make it as a footballer, or there is a chance that you'll have a serious injury and it could end quite quickly. So you need something there, in place, if it doesn't work out."

Craig Mackail-Smith - Brighton & Hove Albion FC

"It can be hard to get a balance between education and football and, to be honest, sometimes the footballer inside you takes over and it's all you think about. You don't really care about education as much as you should when you are a kid because of the attributes you have as a footballer.

I found that I switched off massively because all I was doing was playing football every night, and I felt the only way I was going to become a professional footballer was if I trained and played. I was always waiting for the next football match whether that was at the park or in the school playground at lunchtime. Any time I could use as a practice session was fantastic and that was all I was ever bothered about. I do regret it now but school became more of a social event than an educational event and that was not the teachers' fault; it was my own fault!

What you need to understand is that the majority of young kids all over the country, who set out to become footballers, will not make it! I know it's something you don't want to hear but it's the truth and the reality of the industry. This is why school is so important; coming out with a strong education can really help you push on and achieve great things in life."

Guy Branston (co-author) - a personal reflection

"Regrettably I didn't take too much of an interest at school. I got to the age of 15 and signed for United. I thought I didn't have to worry about anything now.

I've been fortunate really that I've had the career I've had. Looking back it could have gone the other way and I certainly have expressed how important school is to my kids now, and they are pressing through college and university.

It's something you need to do, you have to educate yourself and press on."

Mike Pollitt - Wigan Athletic FC

"Around the time I signed for United I was playing up a bit at school and had an after-school detention. Then I went to a parents' evening once, and basically this teacher just ripped me to shreds in front of my mum and dad, seriously hammered me. I got home and my dad said, "If I get one of those again you're finished at United, I'm not taking you anymore." So that was that, it was like a light switch coming on, and I got my head down."

Ben Amos - Manchester United FC

"I'm all for education. I grew up in Jersey and took my GCSEs, so for me education was a big factor. My mum and dad drilled it into my two sisters and myself - how important education was, and how important it still is today.

I think it can be difficult for kids in academies to focus on education when they probably believe they are going to go on and be the best player in the club and achieve greater things. I can see how it can be very hard for them.

From my point of view I would say to kids, 'you don't know what's going to happen in football', you could go on to be the best player at the club and earn a professional contract and then receive a career threatening injury. I would always advise kids at academies to take their education seriously."

Peter Vincenti - Rochdale AFC

Chapter 8

No one can be 100% sure what the future holds so it's a good idea to have something to fall back on should you fall short and not fulfil the dreams and plans you had set for the rest of your life. Achieving good grades at GCSE, and even in further education, will help give you a good grounding to go on and pursue an alternative career of interest should you not become a professional footballer. Even if you are lucky enough to make it as a pro you must also consider life *after* football. Football won't last forever and most players won't have earned enough money to retire on.

"From a young age, like every other young budding wannabe footballer, I only thought about football and nothing else, which looking back now was daft and stupid. If I had been unfortunate, and not made it, my school grades would not have given me the opportunity to get a good job.

I wish I had worked harder in school and got better grades as I now realise how important they are."

Chris Stokes - Forest Green Rovers FC

"I wasn't a stupid kid but I didn't really try at school and didn't work hard enough to gain any kind of decent qualifications. All I was interested in was football, and between the ages of 25 and 28 it was a real struggle to deal with the transition.

The fact that I didn't know my career would be cut short was difficult, but if you have qualifications and you have to quit football I think it would make it easier for whatever you are going to pursue next. It would probably be an easier transition than the one I had."

Matt Piper - Former Leicester City FC & Sunderland AFC

Enjoy the best of both worlds

In the early years, as your career begins to blossom and you are legally obliged to take part in full-time education, you should try and engage yourself as much as possible in aspects of school that capture your interest. Aspects that you enjoy and have a passion for. You will still have plenty of spare time to dedicate to football outside school.

Choosing football as a career requires a great attitude and for you to be 100% committed - why not take that mentality into your school experience? Why not take that attitude into all aspects of your life?

"I would encourage all young players to focus on their studies just as much as they focus on their football. In my opinion school work is probably more important, because if you focus all your attention on football and don't make it as a pro, you have nothing to fall back on. No grades, no GCSEs, and no qualifications will make finding a job twice as hard as it already is in these modern times.

Having a Plan B is vital and I would recommend to everyone that doing well at school is a must. However, if Plan A is all you've ever wanted, then you'll do anything you can to get it. I worked hard at school, sixth form, and also looked into doing a degree - so now I have good grades and qualifications to fall back on, if I don't continue further in the game."

Jack Baldwin - Peterborough United FC

"Education is also important while you're a scholar because so many scholars get released and you've got to have something to fall back on if it doesn't work out! That way, you can still stay in football, but on the coaching side of things. It's always good to have a backup plan."

Matt Parsons - Plymouth Argyle FC

Chapter 8

> *"I feel that if you're a kid getting distracted from school because of football and consequently are not doing your homework, and teachers are getting on at you, it can affect you in the game as you don't have a clear mind to concentrate and focus solely on football."*
>
> **Peter Vincenti - Rochdale AFC**

> *"I was always bright academically, I made sure I studied well and came out of school with top grades.*
>
> *No matter what I did I always wanted to be the best, whether that was football or whether it was at school. I've just got that attitude."*
>
> **Dan Parslow - York City FC**

Not everyone is academic or comes from a family with an academic background. There are some folks who struggle throughout their education and, frankly, are thankful to get out of school as quickly as possible. If that is the case, it is understandable - but while you're at school you may as well give it your best. You have to attend school anyway! If you apply yourself to the core subjects and other subjects that have a genuine interest for you, you will get something out of school that you can be very proud of.

> *"I would stress the educational side of things. Whatever you are taking at college - do the best you possibly can. You just can't be sure how long your career will be."*
>
> **Peter Vincenti - Rochdale AFC**

Try to be the best you can be at everything you do. It's an attitude that rewards people who stick to it. Live your life with no regrets. Don't be left wondering whether you could have worked or tried harder.

> *"My dad's point of view was you've got to go to school by law, so why not make the most of it? Why don't you just get what you can out of it? It's free education so why wouldn't you? I really took that on-board and worked away and ended up getting good grades. But I'm sure, without my dad's influence, I may not have done so well at school, or had the discipline I have today.*
>
> *I carried on after school as well. I've done English A-level and I'm studying a bit of Spanish, and stuff, so I think it's always something you want to carry on."*
>
> **Ben Amos - Manchester United FC**

Education is becoming increasingly important

Professional football clubs and academies understand how important education is and encourage players to undertake educational programmes, alongside football, during their time with the club.

A lot of clubs offer advice and provide opportunities to move into further education which demonstrates how highly they feel about players continuing their learning and demonstrates how clubs appreciate the value and benefit a good education can have to players.

> *"To be fair the Cardiff setup is very good. They run BTEC's with in-house teachers and stuff, and there were days when we had to do it. If we missed any work we'd have to catch up.*
>
> *So it's not too bad, I mean it's quite limited in terms of the variety of courses you can do, but I suppose that's quite hard as they only have a certain number of facilities."*
>
> **Jonathan Meades - Oxford United FC**

Chapter 8

A large number of players released from professional clubs look to continue their footballing adventure and hope to take advantage of great opportunities available to them in America.

At various educational institutions across a number of States in America they offer you a chance to further your education through a football scholarship, and the great thing is they even pay a large percentage (or even the entire costs) of your tuition and residence fees. However, the scholarship is dependent on your academic as well as footballing performance.

The current state of the economy has seen jobs harder to come by, and that brings a larger number of applicants looking to fill vacant job positions. The greater volume of applicants gives employers more choice and one of the first things that will help them filter through (and discard) applicants will be their educational history.

"My parents had always expressed how important my schoolwork was, and how it would help better my future."

Jonte Smith - Crawley Town FC

Summary

From the moment we enter this world, as a baby, we are constantly learning. Part of this learning is through the formal education system and whilst compulsory school is not everyone's cup of tea - you have to go. So, it makes sense to do the best you can.

It's likely there will be subjects you don't take an interest in, but school institutions must be accommodating to all their pupils; just because you don't have an interest in one subject doesn't mean every other student will share your view. Be respectful of those who enjoy the subject and do the best you can. Besides, how do you know what you do and don't like in life if you haven't tried things?

For every subject you dislike there will also be subjects, and topics you cover, that you have a keen interest and passion for, especially when schooling becomes more flexible and you have to decide what options to pick for your GCSEs. Core subjects like Maths and English will be important throughout your life (you need to understand your contract after all!).

Many subject topics have transferable content and skills that can really aid you on and off the pitch, for example Biology can help you understand biomechanics, English can help with communication on the pitch, and PE can help you develop additional skills and improve your understanding of the body and how it functions.

Learning is something you should try to carry on throughout your life as it keeps you on your toes and allows you to keep moving forward and developing as a person.

It can really pay to work hard and achieve the best grades you can as it can open doors to a whole host of great opportunities.

Top tips from this chapter:

- You have to go to school - so get out of it as much as you can!
- It's unlikely you'll take to every subject, so pick GCSE options that you have a keen interest in.
- It's sensible to try and pick up good GCSEs in as many subjects as you can. You should try and *be the best you can be* in everything you do.
- Enjoy the best of both worlds - you have more than enough time to concentrate on your schoolwork as well as football.
- Qualifications can help you build a bright future, so apply yourself and achieve something you can be proud of.
- Educating yourself and learning are a big part of life after school. If you ever want to play football in Spain, why not learn Spanish? If you want to become a coach, why not take a course in psychology?

9

Success Rates Tell You it's a Tough Industry to Crack

This book isn't designed to put you off following your dream, nor is it designed to pull the wool over your eyes and suggest that - if you work hard and do certain things - you will definitely '100%' make it as a pro footballer.

The idea is to outline the reality that it is a very tough industry and make clear that whilst a relatively small number of people go on to live out a long, successful career as a professional footballer, a much greater number don't make it at all or drop out of the game within a few years of signing professional contracts.

Statistics tell their own story

A report published by the Guardian newspaper, in 2010, outlined statistics taken from the Premier League and Football league, which showed that between 60% and 65% of the 700 or so scholars taken on each year were likely to be rejected at 18. Even half of those who go on to win a full-time contract will not be playing at a professional level by 21.

Similarly a report published by BBC Sport in 2011 referenced the Professional Footballers' Association's (PFA) Chief Executive Gordon Taylor. He pointed out that - of the 600 boys joining Premier League and Football league clubs at the age of 16 - 500 will be out of the professional game by the time they reach the age of 21.

Footballers at 21 years of age who had clubs when they were 16

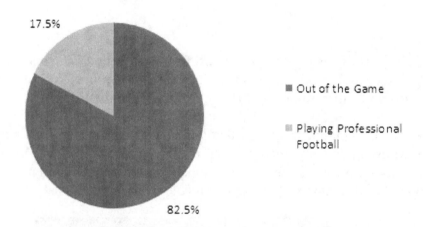

Additionally, in a 2013 TV documentary, former PFA Chairman and ex-professional footballer Clarke Carlisle told a group of young hopefuls looking to make it in the game that, "The likelihood is that you won't make it, you know that don't you? That's the truth. Of all the guys that come into football, there's only 1% that will."

The statistics speak volumes and you can argue they may be slightly dated but it gives you an idea, and a realistic picture, of how difficult it really is. With the increasing number of foreign talents plying their trade in the UK it gets more difficult for home-grown talent to prosper.

Don't let this deter you from aiming to reach for the stars, just be aware of the likelihood of success. It's something that clubs don't always make clear when you reach an academy, and it's understandable to some extent as they don't want to put you off. After all, they cannot foresee exactly how you will develop and progress as a player.

Matt Piper (former pro and current coach of Leicester City FC's U15's) expressed, in an interview, how difficult it can be when delivering information regarding a player's chances of making it:

"I'm quite an honest guy whether that's to young boys, parents, or anyone else. I do, however, think there is a fine line when delivering that kind of information [to youngsters], you don't want to trample all over their dreams and really put them off.

What I do say is the crucial age is between 16 and 18/19, when players are leaving school and they get to that age when they can drive, drink, smoke and girls become more of a factor in life. That is normally the downfall for most great young footballers."

At this point it's worth making it clear, as we have at the beginning of the chapter, that we don't wish to put you off either. Chase the dream with full commitment. There is no harm in that and we very much encourage you to do so. However, it is really important that you are at least aware of how only a small percentage of players make the grade. You need to create an alternative contingency plan so you have something to turn to should you (for whatever reason) not make it as a professional footballer.

It's hard to get there and even harder to stay there

Current and former players who have made it as full time professionals can tell you how hard it is to get into football, but also how hard it is to stay there. They have seen, first hand, the huge number of players that have slipped out of the game during their time in the sport.

> *"I don't know the exact statistics, but take it from me that only something like 5% of kids coming through the academy at YTS level will make it at their club, or another club. It's a tiny amount. So finding that edge over the rest of the group is crucial. You know, what makes you different?*
>
> *If you look at United it's one or two [players], within an age group, that may have a sniff of getting in, out of probably hundreds from a young age that have fallen out of the game since."*

Ben Amos - Manchester United FC

> *"The U16's level is the first jump up into a scholarship, and there were probably about 14-16 people to an age group. Around 6-10 get a scholarship and that's when you train every day, you're continuing your education, and you're really part of the club. You're also on a little payroll as well. You do your two-year scholarship and then it's the big jump up to professional football.*
>
> *From my age group there must have been about 10 of us, four got professional contracts and are still in the game three years on, which is rare for that to happen; but I think, to be fair, this was because we always had a really strong age group.*
>
> *When I was a second year scholar, the age group below (who were first year scholars) - I don't think any of them play professional football now."*

Jonathan Meades - Oxford United FC

"From when I was in the youth team, aged 16-19, only three of us out of around 40 players are in the full time professional game. Stats say that from a squad of 20 players only one or two will actually stay in the game, and that's not even at the football club you're at.

The fact that football is such a big business now means some managers tend to shy away from giving youngsters a chance. They would rather go with someone who has been there, and done it, and has more experience, so they know what they are getting.

I think the biggest thing the FA and any footballing body need to do is get into these academies from an early age and spell it out - in black and white - that only a few of you are going to make it. The sooner people see the reality of it, the sooner they can prepare a plan B."

Dan Parslow - York City FC

"The Palace academy, at the time I was there, was sought after. A lot of players were making the grade and getting into the first team. Out of my under-16s team, which was a team that lost nine games in two seasons, there are only five lads playing in the Football League or Premier league and one of those boys didn't even get a scholarship at Palace. Most of the lads ended up in non-league, then dropped out altogether, or just found something else that was for them."

Matt Fish - Gillingham FC

"Unfortunately there are lots of people that don't make it as footballers and careers don't last past playing in academies. From the academy group I was in at Bristol city, which had about 25 people, only 3 people including myself are still playing today.

These numbers are roughly the same in all other academies. They say only one person from each academy age group will go on to make a living in football. With this in mind it's hugely important to have a back up plan just in case you're one of the 24/25 that don't make it."

Chris Stokes - Forest Green Rovers FC

"My year included Scott Parker, Stuart Taylor and Alan Smith. The year above included Michael Owen and Wes Brown, and the year below included Joe Cole.

For all those big names the vast majority were out of football within five years which is a lesson in itself as to how hard becoming a footballer, and staying there, really is."

Kevin Nicholson - Torquay United FC

"They called my age group a 'golden era' and the coaches used to talk about that a lot. When we were 13/14 we were beating Manchester United's and Chelsea's academy sides and for a club like Leicester City it was pretty much unheard of.

Out of that 18-man squad, who all stayed together and all received youth team contracts, four made it. From the four that progressed into the first team, there are only two that are still playing and those are hugely impressive figures.

Since I made it into the first team squad in 2001, 13 years ago, I'd say there have been no more than 12 boys who have gone on to the first team and stayed with the club for a substantial period of time. So, 12 lads in 13 years."

Matt Piper - Former-Leicester City FC & Sunderland AFC

"I think it can be difficult for youngsters with the small success rate that comes out of academies. A lot of players can go by the wayside, and lose belief and confidence in themselves, and go play non-league football.

I think there are a few clubs, one of them is Dagenham and the other is Peterborough, who are looking to the non-league to find a few gems, and I think if more clubs did that (and helped players that have come out of academies and gone into non-league) it will provide great opportunities for more players. You will then hear of a lot more success stories."

Craig Mackail-Smith - Brighton & Hove Albion FC

Summary

The figures don't make for encouraging reading, and the Chief Executive of the Professional Footballers Association (PFA) Gordon Taylor acknowledges that it's not good enough and needs to be addressed. He has said, "If it was a university of football, with our success rates, we would have been closed down by now, because it's just not good enough."

Over the years, an increase in the number of foreign players in the Premier League has made it very difficult for homegrown talent to make it in the top tier of English football.

The Premier League has taken action to attempt to improve the chances of homegrown talent with the introduction of the 'home-grown' rule under which a 25 man Premier League squad must include at least eight home-grown players.

It's a start but everyone including the PFA knows there's a long way to go:

"It's the first step. I think the second step needs to be the rule should apply to those on the field," said PFA chief Gordon Taylor.

A 'home-grown' player is defined as a player who has trained with an English or Welsh team for three or more years between the ages of 16 and 21, so does not necessarily have to even be English or British. Taylor believes that there should be at least four home-grown players in every starting XI.

Don't let this chapter be a reason to stop chasing your dream. Simply use this chapter as an eye-opener to the reality of the success rates attached to the football industry. Use the information as encouragement to think about alternatives. Explore other options just in case you do not make it as a professional.

Top tips from this chapter:

- Don't let the figures, above, stop you from chasing your dream. *You* can still be that player that makes it.
- Be aware that a professional career is extremely difficult to obtain though, so be wise and have an alternative interest to pursue should you not succeed in the game.

10

It's Wise to have Something to Fall Back On

What happens if you join the great number of young footballing prospects that don't live out full careers as a professional footballer? Clearly, it would be advisable to have an alternative career choice, or interest, to turn to.

It can be difficult knowing what you want

At any age it can be hard to know what you want to do with your life. But this can be especially difficult at a young age, as you may not fully understand what a job really involves. Not knowing what you want to do - after being let go by a club or having your career cut short - can really have a negative effect and get you down.

As you near 16 some of you may be fortunate enough to have a rough idea of what industry you would like to enter. You might not have a specific job role in mind but, for instance, you may know you want to do something in sport, something business related, or maybe you want to do something hands on and pick up a trade like an electrician or plumber. You may even wish to move into higher education and enrol at a university. It can be a case of trial and error to work out what job role or future best suits you.

> *"I've always said I'd have been a sports journalist, but I've seen how difficult that is to get into now. My ex-girlfriend and friends wanted to get into it and it's very competitive. I was good at English but I'm not sure I was that good; you've got to be the best of the best in that field.*
>
> *I don't know exactly what I would have done, but I'm sure I would have liked to stay in football somehow. I just made sure I had a bit of grounding with my GCSEs and my A-level to go on and do something."*
>
> **Ben Amos - Manchester United FC**

Try having a back up plan

Your back up career doesn't have to be something mundane and boring, find something you are passionate about, not something you're told to do or something you do because you don't feel you are capable of doing anything better. You're in work for a long time so don't waste it doing something you hate! Find something you enjoy, which you look forward to when you wake up in the morning.

> *"I had a backup plan in place because of the GCSEs that I had acquired. If I was not playing football I'd be studying to be an accountant."*
>
> **Jonte Smith - Crawley Town FC**

"I went to university but I still very much believed that I would be a professional footballer. However, if I had fallen out of the game I think I would have probably become a PE teacher.

I would have done a postgrad qualification. I'd already done a placement as a PE teacher that I enjoyed, so would have probably carried that on. But it's hard to say, to be honest, because I certainly looked to do something involved with sport. I would possibly have looked at different avenues and maybe even tried to go to university in America and play out there."

Neill Collins - Sheffield United FC

"If I hadn't found football I was always looking to go into the army, although when I was released by Crystal Palace I went down into non-league football and trained as a fitness instructor and then went on to be a personal trainer. So I played part-time football and worked part-time in a gym. This was a very good life as I had the best of both worlds."

Matt Fish - Gillingham FC

"Before signing my first professional contract at Hartlepool United, I was all ready to go to university to study physiotherapy. I was enrolled on the course, I had my student loans sorted, and I had my student accommodation sorted out. I then went on trial at Hartlepool a few weeks before heading off to university, which was when I was successful and signed as a pro."

Jack Baldwin - Peterborough United FC

"I had gone away to university for three years and had got my degree in Business and Sports Science, and was offered a job in the finance industry, which is what I had been studying.

I was then offered the trial at Millwall and consequently signed professionally for them."

Peter Vincenti - Rochdale AFC

> *"I did my A levels and then I went to college and studied a BTEC National Diploma in Sports Science and I was ready to go to university before I joined Dagenham.*
>
> *It was a case of deciding what side of sport I wanted to be in; whether it was physiotherapy, or actually involved in team rehabilitation or strength and conditioning.*
>
> *I had a plan in that sense. I obviously had great belief that I could be a professional footballer, but I wanted to make sure I had my qualifications in case I was to have a serious injury. So, it was there for back up."*
>
> **Craig Mackail-Smith - Brighton & Hove Albion FC**

It's inadvisable to put all your eggs in one basket and not consider anything other than playing football for a living. Anything - from an injury to a lack of development - can prevent you achieving your ambition. It's hard enough dealing with the realization that you won't become or continue to be a footballer, but it can be a whole lot worse if you haven't considered what you'll do next.

> *"You know what it can be like. You're a young lad and you've just signed for Manchester United, nothing else really matters.*
>
> *Luckily it worked out and I've had a long career, but thinking like that couldn't be any further from the truth. You're only one kick away from a major injury and having to finish in the game. I would certainly advise any players, now, not to put all your eggs in one basket in the hope of becoming a footballer. It is a crazy thing to do."*
>
> **Mike Pollitt - Wigan Athletic FC**

"I had no plan in place and then, out-of-the-blue, an injury meant I had to quit football. This is when it hits you and you realize you haven't got a clue what you are going to do.

I went through a few months of watching TV everyday as I was still living off the money I had earned as a footballer, and then reality hits you and you realize you have to do something else with your life. The most frustrating thing for me was not knowing what I wanted to do.

If I had read a book like this one, and there was a story about a lad who only wanted to be a footballer since he was eight years old, and he achieves his dream and gets his big move and gets paid thousands and thousands of pounds a week, and lives in big houses and drives nice cars and all of a sudden 'Bang' an injury comes and that's it all taken away within 3-4 years, and he has spent and lost almost everything – that's me! All because there wasn't a plan there from the start; I'm not saying it would have definitely worked for me but it could have helped."

Matt Piper - Former Leicester City FC & Sunderland AFC

Summary

Chase every boys dream of becoming a footballer and go for it with everything you have got. That's what you should do. But there is no harm in having a backup plan. Many professional players had backup plans in place should they have failed to make it. A backup plan shouldn't reduce your drive to make it in the game but simply better prepare you if unfortunate circumstances make it impossible to be a full time footballer.

Top tips from this chapter:

- It can be difficult to know exactly what else you'd like to do after football, so explore a number of alternative avenues and find one that suits you.
- It can be a demoralizing and traumatic time if you realize you won't make it, especially if you have no backup plan. So set something up, whilst you are training to become a footballer, just in case.
- Find something that interests you, and which you have a passion for. There are lots of other jobs in football besides playing.

11

Attention Parents! You Have a Huge Role to Play

Parents and close family are a vital component in any young aspiring footballer's life, especially in the early days. Young players are hugely reliant on their parents, and look to them for advice and guidance. Without their support, encouragement, and transportation it would be almost impossible for a young child to push on and take opportunities as they arise.

Encouragement, Guidance and Support

As a child grows up and takes their first steps into the footballing world they can be very vulnerable and, accordingly, need guidance and supervision from their parents.

What they learn from their parents will be taken forward as they develop and it is important that any parental guidance is helpful, realistic, and supportive. The 'right advice' can put a child on the right track and, in the same way, bad advice can prove detrimental and inhibit a person's ability to progress.

The obvious place for a parent to start is by ensuring their child knows the difference between right and wrong; this can involve anything from lifestyle choices to work ethic to social behaviour to nutritional advice and much more.

Chapter 11

Sometimes it can be a case of telling a child what they *need to hear* and maybe not what they *want to hear*. At the time this may not go down well so it is important to spell out *why* any advice is given and the good intentions behind any advice. A parent should not seek to lecture a youngster; engage in a dialogue that explores the issues together. Message, meaning, and impact will be much stronger when undertaken in a collaborative manner.

"I think I had a good balance. My dad would say to me sometimes, "It would be a crime with your talent if you don't make it," so I did feel a bit of pressure from my father in that respect. Don't get me wrong, he wasn't like what I've read about the Williams sisters' dad in tennis where he had them out training until midnight. He was nothing like that but he would be the one that put that slight bit of pressure on me, telling me to not go out and trying to keep me on track to how we thought a professional footballer should be brought up.

Whereas my mum obviously wanted me to make it but she also wanted me to enjoy growing up and it wasn't all about football. She sometimes used to say I should go to some of those parties, that I never went to, and enjoy myself.

So I had a mix between the two and when one got too much I could always go to my other parent and get some information and advice from them to counterbalance what the other one was saying.

Sometimes I look at it and think my mum would have let me do anything I wanted, which wouldn't have been good, whereas my dad hardly let me do anything and that's not too good either. So the balance between the two I felt provided me with a good upbringing."

Matt Piper - Former Leicester City FC & Sunderland AFC

"My dad was always very supportive but at the same time was my biggest critic, he didn't always tell me what I wanted to hear but he was very honest with me and when I had a bad game, or if I'd done something not quite right, he would tell me and he still does now. It wasn't necessarily what I wanted to hear but it was advice and feedback I trusted and I think it helped me a great deal."

Peter Vincenti - Rochdale AFC

Parents need to remember: first and foremost *be a parent*. Appreciate your child's interests and be supportive in every aspect of your child's life.

Football specific advice should be used sparingly if a parent lacks the relevant experience and expertise in the game. It's important to assess how commendable and reliable any footballing advice is; a lot of people claim to know the game inside out!

"Throughout all the setbacks and good times, my family have always been there for me with good advice and even a shoulder to cry on at times! Which I think you need. It's a massive part of why I am where I am (still in the game)."

Matt Parsons - Plymouth Argyle FC

"My dad was originally from Scotland and was a good footballer when he was a kid. He moved to Jersey from a young age and he actually managed the Jersey Island football team, so he's knowledgeable in football and would always help me growing up, would pass on advice, and it's still advice I trust to this day. Both my parents have been great and really supportive and get over to the UK to watch me play as much as they can."

Peter Vincenti - Rochdale AFC

Bringing a child up with a lifestyle and in an atmosphere that accommodates football's requirements will give that child a platform to go on and be the best they can be.

"It's important to have the knowledge within the family to encourage kids to live their lives a certain way. It can be difficult as kids may not wish to live the way you are encouraging them to; nevertheless providing advice and highlighting the benefits that come from adopting a certain regime can help persuade a youngster that it's the right lifestyle for them.

Consequently, adopting the right lifestyle will have huge benefits in the long run and can leave a child better equipped to deal with more intense training as they grow up. They need to be in a physical condition and frame of mind to handle it."

Guy Branston (co-author) - a personal reflection

There are also other little things parents can do. For example, parents can help tackle dehydration. Parents should remain conscious of their lads coming home and not rehydrating by drinking enough water. As a result they could return to training having not recovered properly and suffer muscle spasms.

Encourage a happy medium

Football is full of mixed emotions and continuous cycles of highs and lows. It is vitally important a young player doesn't get carried away - possibly as a result of receiving unjustified or over-the-top praise that can (in some instances) be a setup for huge disappointment.

This said it is equally important not to allow a child to get too down and disappointed either; in other words don't get carried away by the highs, but also don't get too down hearted and despondent with the lows. Provide a happy medium. Keep a child grounded and realistic. This can really help to avoid complacency moving forward.

"My dad would always be the first to say that you can never ever tell if someone will definitely make it. What he would say is, "If you do this or do that, you are good enough, and you'll give yourself the best possible chance." He never made me expectant, never made me think that I had the God-given right to make it.

He probably took as much pride in me playing my first game for Queens Park in the Scottish 3rd division than anything because, at the time, he probably thought it might be the highest I'd ever go, as you just don't know.

He would always say, "If you keep doing the right things, you'll have a chance." He would never put any pressure on me but would always know the right times to push me.

I think there's another thing; you do get pushy parents and I think you need that pushiness sometimes because things aren't good enough - whether it comes from your mum and dad or your coach. I was quite fortunate in that respect."

Neill Collins - Sheffield United FC

"You can see if people get excited or down, it's not rocket science. If a child is excited and can't contain his emotions and is bouncing about, you can recognise it. The same way you can see a child who is down and upset over the smallest of things.

It's about bringing up a child who is able to handle his emotions but also able to manage the situations that occur quite regularly in football. It's such an up and down sport.

You've got to find your own methods in how to deal with youngsters. We see it time after time in the game where a young player bursts onto the scene. He is fantastic for six months and then dips very quickly, and that can be because the excitement around him sometimes gets into his head and he loses his focus, his tempo, and his work rate. He thinks he's made it.

Parents need to understand that footballing success is ultimately about consistency. A player has to be constantly working hard at their game."

Guy Branston (co-author) - a personal reflection

Chapter 11

Additional pressure is not helpful

Pressure is something that is part and parcel of the footballing environment. As expectation levels grow (from a variety of people including friends, family, coaches, clubs, managers and fans) it's likely a player's expectancy levels will increase.

A parent should avoid putting unnecessary pressure on their child. Some parents dreamt of becoming a professional footballer, but didn't make it, and are so fixated with the idea of professional football that they overly pressure their child to live out the dream they never fulfilled.

"The pressure on a child to live the dream that the parent didn't manage can be really destructive. It puts unfair pressure on a kid, without the parent even realizing.

A child should have the freedom to decide what they enjoy and what they would like to pursue. Parents should try to be as supportive as possible whatever path they choose. Parents should guide, not control."

Guy Branston (co-author) - a personal reflection

"My advice to parents would be to support your child as much as you can, but don't force them. Obviously there are situations where you have to help them out and try giving them a bit of a push but if, after a while, they're not enjoying it, don't force them to do it. Luckily, I never had that.

Also screaming from the side-line at your kid, from a young age, really doesn't benefit them at all. Don't do it when they are playing. Just have a little word with them off the pitch in a constructive way rather than shouting at them."

Jonathan Meades - Oxford United FC

"My parents weren't pushy at all; they just wanted me to be the best I could be."

Dan Parslow - York City FC

"My parents' advice was to just enjoy it. I'm lucky enough to have grown up with two parents who are very, very supportive of myself and my two sisters. They wanted me and my two sisters to be individuals and be whatever we wanted to be.

They never used to force anything on us. The only thing they really stressed was the educational side of things and whatever we decided to do they would support us."

Peter Vincenti - Rochdale AFC

"I was very lucky, my parents never pushed me to do something I didn't want to do, and they were always supporting me.

My dad was probably more interested in me getting my education first, than actually making it as a professional footballer.

I think parents play a massive role. For some parents it's tough because they just see the professional side of it and they want their kids to become a professional footballer so badly that they kind of neglect the educational part.

If their young lads are at clubs, I think it's down to the parents to help them get something together so they have something in place after football."

Craig Mackail-Smith - Brighton & Hove Albion FC

"Kids start playing football at seven or eight years old these days and at that tender age they should participate in football for fun and enjoyment and nothing else. Pressure shouldn't be exerted on them.

As much as you want to push your kid and introduce him to the pressure of being a footballer early on, it is only a game at a young age. It's about learning, it's about enjoyment, and producing a player that loves football all his life. So the pleasure level has to be high, as well as the excitement level, to help motivate a youngster to go training every day.

I still have that fun factor now. The drive to carry on training at 35 and I want to train hard because I can not only see the rewards, but I really enjoy the rewards."

Guy Branston (co-author) - a personal reflection

Requires dedication: financially and with time

A young lad's decision to pursue a career in football requires the undivided support of parents and a dedication to do *whatever you can* to give your child the best possible opportunities. This can involve a lot of travelling and consequently a financial outlay. But without your support, encouragement, and willingness to travel, your child's ability to chase their dream becomes harder. Remember, your support will be something your child will always appreciate and never forget.

"The role of parents is very important. Without the parents and families within the game - there wouldn't be a game! Taking a player to football every day, dropping them off, and picking them up. What I remember, as a kid, is my stepfather driving me to Nottingham to play for Notts County and train there.

He was constantly on the go to Nottingham to give me the opportunity to play for a professional football club. It is obviously something I am very thankful for. Without his support I would never have had the chance to pursue my dream."

Guy Branston (co-author) - a personal reflection

> *"I'd say my mum and dad gave the biggest sacrifice; driving me to training three or four days a week and driving me all over the country for the games, even though they both had full time jobs. Without them taking me everywhere, and putting that time and effort in, I wouldn't be where I am today."*

Ben Amos - Manchester United FC

> *"The role my parents played was huge, taxiing me everywhere for trials and games and then coming to support me each week. The support and guidance they showed me throughout, whilst respecting the coaching and not overstepping their mark, was a huge factor in my success."*

Kevin Nicholson - Torquay United FC

> *"My parents were really good to me; I literally had no pressure on me whatsoever, in any situation.*
>
> *It's obviously a lot of commitment from them. I was training or playing 20 minutes away, four times a week, and even if that's just lifts - sometimes they would have to come and stay to watch. So, it's a lot of commitment. But they never once turned around and said 'you better make it'."*

Jonathan Meades - Oxford United FC

Club academies have developed and improved over the years and if a child is part of an academy setup they are in a great environment to prosper, with professional coaches, and nutritional and lifestyle advice. Some academies even provide transportation.

Academies provide an alternative source of advice and guidance that, in some cases, can be more relevant. After all, it comes from personnel who are qualified and well placed to give reliable industry-specific advice.

> *"The game has changed so much over the years, and the clubs now have these sports scientists, physios, strength and conditioning coaches; you have everybody you need to look after you.*
>
> *It was different back then. The food side of it wasn't as serious and well documented as it is these days.*
>
> *People now advise you what to eat and what to drink, it's incredible really. Sometimes we do like to cheat now and then and will have a chinese, or whatever, but in general we try to look after ourselves and the clubs provide the food, give advice, and offer supplements, so you'd be a fool not to take it on-board."*
>
> **Mike Pollitt - Wigan Athletic FC**

> *"I am an academy coach at Leicester City now and I know the information we give the kids is excellent. The club wants to drill into the kids, early, that alcohol is no good for you, and smoking is no good for you. They also advise about good nutrition to get players into good habits."*
>
> **Matt Piper - Former Leicester City FC & Sunderland AFC**

In the case of players that take an alternative route into the professional game it can sometimes be difficult to find reliable football specific advice.

> *"If you're within an academy; I think you do receive really good advice from the coaches. Outside of that it is tough though.*
>
> *You need to take bits of advice from those around you and I think the Internet is a great tool for helping now. Especially watching YouTube videos or finding information through a Google search. They are a great point of call if you don't have coaches and football experts around you."*
>
> **Craig Mackail-Smith - Brighton & Hove Albion FC**

Being part of an academy that provides transport can also help reduce the financial outlay attached to travelling that some families simply cannot afford.

"When I signed for United my dad started to come. Before that, at schoolboy level, I was having to borrow lifts off people to get from A to B.

My parents were always interested to see how I got on, but it was difficult because my mum and dad never really had a car so they couldn't really run me around.

I do the opposite now. I've got two boys now and I have a car and run them about everywhere and that's because I have the chance to do so. It was difficult when I was growing up because we didn't really have that much money and there were five children in the house, so it was hard sometimes to get us all about.

When I was playing regularly all the time my mum and dad were coming to all the games, as they could get about. They were quite proud really and really supportive."

Mike Pollitt - Wigan Athletic FC

All in all, it is *the people around a youngster* who prove so important in helping that person make it.

> *"Academies offer advice to help develop all-round players both within football and outside as well. Top academies are fantastic with the depth of advice they offer. They have welfare officers (people to talk to if there are problems in the family), and will sometimes provide transport to get players to training and games.*
>
> *These are modern day academies. I remember catching four buses to get to the academy at Leicester City, and that was when I was an apprentice, and that was three times a week. My parents couldn't afford to keep driving me around as it was becoming expensive. Nowadays the academies bend over backwards for you if you're a talented player because they want you in their academy and at their football club.*
>
> *When I hear parents worrying about their kid/s joining academies because all they want is for their kid/s to enjoy their football, I think - a kid will enjoy his football more in the academy environment. He gets to play on nice pitches and work with nice people and great coaches who are qualified and trained in the art of looking after certain age groups."*
>
> **Guy Branston (co-author) - a personal reflection**

Summary

Becoming a parent and following a child as they grow and develop is a great thing and provides many proud moments in life. Everyone has their own parenting methods; there is no specific 'best' way.

With a football mad son - support, advice and guidance are paramount in allowing that child to progress. These actions will help put them in a position to receive opportunities that can take them to the next level.

Football is full of ups and downs, so it is vital to be honest with a child and provide them with a happy medium that grounds them. Do not allow them to get carried away with the highs, and do not allow them to become discouraged by the lows.

Top tips from this chapter:

- Be supportive of a child's interests.
- Make clear the differences between good and bad habits that can help or hinder someone in the footballing world.
- Promote and encourage a happy medium.
- Enjoyment is the most important thing.
- Providing additional pressure can be a massive hindrance.
- Offer advice but ultimately allow youngsters to make their own decisions. Try not to dictate their lives and force them into things they don't want to do.
- Your son needs you! Without parental commitment and dedication, a footballer will not be able to progress and seize the chance of fulfilling their dream of becoming a professional footballer.

12

Football is a Short Career

There are no guarantees in football and with relatively short-term contracts involved it is really difficult to establish how long you will have in the game. You would consider yourself to be very fortunate to have played professional football for anything more than 15 years, but in comparison to other careers – this is not long.

Football can end at any point and be precipitated by anything from a dip in form to an injury or even in some cases (towards the later stages of your career) a loss of love for the game. Whatever the cause, you can find yourself in a position where you must re-evaluate your circumstances and ask 'what's next'?

"If you're successful and have a good career in football, it is still a very short career - on average retiring at 35/36 - and it is very rare in lower league football that you will earn enough money to retire on. Therefore it is very important to have a career to go into after playing football, such as teaching, physiotherapy, or sports science to name a few."

Jack Baldwin - Peterborough United FC

Chapter 12

Think about life after football

You can never be sure when it will be time to hang up your boots for good and finish your footballing career, so enjoy every game and training session as though it is your last.

Although you will train very hard and do a lot of intense training sessions, whilst you are a professional footballer, you will be given time to rest and this is a great opportunity to explore what you are going to do after your playing days are over.

It's tough though. You've worked so hard to make it in the game and all you want to do is live in the moment and concentrate solely on football. That's okay but you would have known, from the start, that a footballing career doesn't go on forever…

The earlier you begin to plan for life after football the better, as you can't be sure exactly when it will end.

"My career finished at 25 through injury.

I'm well over it now but for three or four years after I finished I was a bit of a lost soul, to be honest, because all I had wanted to do was play football since I was eight years old. I reached my dream playing in the first team at Leicester City. I was then sold to Sunderland for big money (£3.5 Million), and I was a regular week-in week-out in the Premier League. Then, within the four years I was at Sunderland, that dream was over and I had to find something else to do.

I had no plan in place and then had to quit. This is when it hits you and you haven't got a clue what you are going to do.

You go from being a professional footballer for 6 to 7 years to suddenly doing nothing; it was a real shock."

Matt Piper - Former Leicester City FC & Sunderland AFC

> *"I haven't got a massive back up in place at the moment but I'm definitely going to look into it. Even the current injury puts it into perspective. I'm thinking of doing a course while I'm doing my football, like a physiotherapy course. I'm actually looking into that at the moment."*

Jonathan Meades - Oxford United FC

> *"After my playing career, I'd definitely look into an alternative career in football, whether it's coaching or agency work of some sort. I haven't decided just yet. But my love for the game is so strong, I don't think I'd ever not see it as a massive part of my life."*

Matt Parsons - Plymouth Argyle FC

> *"A lot of people say 'why don't you become a coach?', the problem is that's becoming a very crowded market when you come out of the game. The playing side of the game is very tough, but it's just as difficult to get involved with a pro club on the coaching side of things.*
>
> *I think about life after football all the time. It's something I've been doing now for the last 25 years and I would like to stay in the game if possible.*
>
> *I've been doing all my coaching badges and have my UEFA A license in the summer, so hopefully I can move into goalkeeper coaching.*
>
> *Unwisely I haven't really thought about being outside the game, so hopefully I can continue in the game and help the next generation."*

Mike Pollitt - Wigan Athletic FC

You may not be able to prepare yourself for the emotions attached with hanging up your boots, after running out onto that field for the last time, but you can prepare yourself to move straight into your next career or venture.

Chapter 12

> *"I think the difficult thing with thinking about life after football is that you don't know how it is going to affect you until you're not turning up to training on a Monday morning. I mean, some of these players would have done it for 20 years and that's all they would have done.*
>
> *So I think the sooner you start preparing yourself for life after football, the better."*
>
> **Dan Parslow - York City FC**

> *"You get to the point where you understand football is over and that's gone, but now what?*
>
> *I've done some work with the PFA on not having anything in place before finishing football because of what happened to me and I don't mind admitting it.*
>
> *Because I didn't know what to do next, it slowly depressed me and within a year or two that depression was obviously a lot deeper. Then you look for things that give you some kind of excitement or adrenaline, when nothing else is there and I took to drink and gambling and within two years of finishing my football career, I actually had to go to rehab because of drink. I went to the Tony Adams clinic called 'Sporting Chance' which he set up because he had his problems with gambling and drinking. That's what happened to me, all because I didn't have something in place for when I had to quit football.*
>
> *People think once they've made it - that's it. Even people that are retiring at old ages like 35/36 (and I've talked to ex-pros) they go through the same troubles as I did and they've had a full career. But there's something missing after football because they haven't put a plan in place for when they do finish, and it is tough."*
>
> **Matt Piper - Former Leicester City FC & Sunderland AFC**

"It is something you need to prepare for. You hear about the depression side of things so much. Players are now coming out and saying they are depressed and there is a lot more awareness being raised.

With me I'm obviously not playing as regularly but I'm going through the transition slowly. I've not just, all of a sudden, completely stopped.

I've been involved with Wigan now for nine years and I've gone from playing quite regularly to slowly not playing and I think it's helped me a little bit doing it that way. It helps prepare you that little bit more."

Mike Pollitt - Wigan Athletic FC

"Many pro footballers haven't got a clue what they will do when they finish because it is all they know."

Matt Fish - Gillingham FC

"I think it's got a bit of a stigma – planning for life after football. I don't think youngsters want to be associated with doing it and want to be seen to be concentrating on their football. A lot of people seem to think that, while they are so young, it's something they will do after football. But I think it's definitely better to do it while you're playing football, as you have the time to do it. So, you may as well."

Jonathan Meades - Oxford United FC

Financial Planning

A lot of people outside football think every single professional footballer, regardless of what level they play, lives a life that consists of expensive cars, lavish houses and bags and bags of money that will keep them going long after football. This is simply not the case for the majority of footballers.

Regular starting players who play in the top tier of English football (Premier

League) and players at the top end of the Championship may be in a position where money isn't an issue and they will be comfortable long after retirement. But this assumes they were sensible with their money. If a player was not sensible, or played in the lower tiers of the game, income will have to be found.

Even long term servants in the Premier League can struggle when they retire. It can be difficult to avoid being wasteful and erratic with your money when there are people around you with the latest cars, designer clothes, and technology. Over time a high spending lifestyle can really come back to haunt you. This is where financial planning and speaking to the right people - regarding financial management - can really help.

"A lot of people say, once you're playing in the Premier League, it's sort of like winning the lottery. You think 'I'm never going to have to worry about money again as long as I'm sensible with it'.

Obviously where it catches a lot of people out is when you live to your circumstances. For instance, if you're earning £10,000 a week you are probably spending £8,000 on cars, designer clothes, and expensive jewellery for your missus.

I'm not painting everyone with the same brush because some people do earn £10,000 a week and spend £1,500 and start putting the rest into assets and things like that, but there are a lot of people, when they start earning better money, who start living that better life. And it does catch you out.

In the dressing room I don't feel you are put under pressure necessarily to have the latest car, or technology, but it becomes human nature when you are in the Premier League. You come into the ground with your nice sensible car and you see someone else come in with a Lamborghini; you think I must be earning the same sort of money as him. It happened to me. I said to myself: 'I will be nice and sensible,' and then one of your mates comes in with a new car or some new technology, and you think 'I want one of them'. Because you have the money you do it. That's what the environment can do to your mentality!"

Matt Piper - Former Leicester City FC & Sunderland AFC

> *"I know players who have been in the Premiership for five or six years and who are skint. It's one of those things. You spend your money as it comes and you enjoy yourself. You're a young lad, you buy cars, you have the latest gadgets. Help with understanding finances is something you're not really hooked up with.*
>
> *I wish I had some more guidance as a youngster because I'd be a lot better off than I am now and I've had 20 years in the game. I'm not saying I am uncomfortable... I would just have more than I currently have. It's about being wise enough to be switched on, and getting yourself organized early.*
>
> *Admittedly money does come to you quite quickly but it also ends very quickly. I would always say have short-term, medium-term, and long-term money put away so you are covered for every eventuality, and can get by until you find an alternative income stream."*
>
> **Guy Branston (co-author) - a personal reflection**

Summary

Getting organised and looking at life beyond football is of huge benefit to any footballer. It can soften the disappointment of finishing in the game and will help keep your mind occupied in the absence of football. You do not need to just prepare career choices for after football, you also need to determine what lifestyle choices you are going to make.

Live in the moment, but always keep one eye on the future; an alternative career and careful financial planning whilst in the game will set you up nicely for a bright enjoyable future after football.

> *"You should always plan to a certain extent. Focus on your football when you are playing it but when you go home, and switch off and do other things, look at other avenues you are interested in. Take the time to educate yourself, take the time to try different things."*
>
> **Guy Branston (co-author) - a personal reflection**

Top tips from this chapter:

- The earlier you plan for life after football the easier you will find the transition.
- Explore different avenues and research alternative industries in your spare time to help identify things you enjoy and have a passion for.
- Revenue from football comes quickly but also ends quickly, so be sensible and set yourself up for life after the game.

13

There is So Much to Love about being a Footballer

We've discussed and outlined the reality of football, its competitive nature, and the toughness of the industry, but there is no denying the fact that playing football is a great career (or hobby) that brings many enjoyable and unforgettable moments to a large number of individuals across the UK and entire world.

Unforgettable Experiences

"I've had loads of fun experiences whilst being a footballer. Where do you start?

The biggest thing for me, as a footballer, was the reality of finally becoming one. I found it fantastic signing my first pro contract. I went in and spoke to the manager about it, not thinking that I'd got one, but I was playing for the reserves as an apprentice and was doing really well. I kind of knew I was doing something right on the pitch when the pros started talking to me about getting an agent and stuff like that.

It was a time where really positive things were happening in my life. Every day I was waking up excited to go to training, looking forward to go to a job that was filled with excitement and borderline anxiety. Every day was so different and every day was so exciting.

(continued) *All the experiences I had early in my career were very positive: making the first team coach trip, travelling with the first team, and being involved with them going to America. Having the opportunity to mix with the people I grew up watching and having them now see me as a team mate and an associate. I was playing cards with them on the bus and going out and socializing with them, having dinner with them.*

You're 17/18 and you're having dinner with someone you looked up to. The banter is flying, you are fully involved. You get to line up next to your hero who, for me growing up, was Steve Walsh. I'm looking at him thinking - this is a bit eerie. I was a little star struck, but you've obviously got to get over that and play well to impress him, or he's going to start screaming at you.

It was also a great experience going on loan for the first time, looking to make your mark and progress. At the time that was with Rushden and Diamonds and I met two of my best mates there and they are still my best mates now.

Then going to Colchester and winning promotion in my first full year as a pro. I went to sign for Colchester and we were 10th in the league and 15 points off the play offs. We made the play offs and ended up winning promotion, and I played in the play off final that season.

There are so many fun and enjoyable experiences in football but it would take me hours to talk about them all!"

Guy Branston (co-author) - a personal reflection

"Whilst I've had limited opportunities I will never forget some of the experiences I've had over the years. Playing in the Champions League and Premier League for Manchester United were things that I truly had dreamt of as a boy, and these have been my highlights so far. Added to that I have enjoyed some unbelievable trips on pre-season tours, spending weeks at a time with the best players in the world."

Ben Amos - Manchester United FC

"There are too many experiences to talk about and some of the stories are probably even too rude. At the club I play for we have to drive to the training ground in our cars and numerous times someone's car has been taken after training, and driven back to the ground, and parked in the gaffer's space.

Many items of clothing have been hung up in the changing room from bad clobber to dirty pants.

Lights go off in the boot room and boots are being flung around, cold buckets of ice chucked over lads in the shower, and stitching people's cars when they leave, or when they have done something to you.

Once we stitched the physio's car up with foam burst shower gel that foams up when it gets wet; when he was driving home it started raining and he almost crashed on the motorway, funny but also very dangerous.

No one will understand the banter and fun and games that go on unless you are involved in it. This is what most pros miss when they retire."

Matt Fish - Gillingham FC

"It is difficult to pinpoint something when you're involved in it everyday. Fun experiences I've had are just simple things like the banter and the camaraderie in the dressing room with the lads. Silly things that happen in training, initiations you have to go through at a new club.

There have been times when we've had a good result, a cup run, promotion, and the team has gone out to celebrate. These have always provided fond memories."

Peter Vincenti - Rochdale AFC

Chapter 13

"I've had so many fun experiences and memories through football. From the moment I joined my local team, Cascade Youth Club, when we travelled the region all summer playing in many mini-football tournaments (winning most of them), again with some really good friends.

I was fortunate to get spotted for my boyhood team, Cardiff City, although it's a shame that I didn't make a senior appearance having been there from the age of 12 through to 20.

I loved my time as a YTS, it made me grow up quickly, being thrown into a competitive football environment. I learned some amazing life skills and matured a lot during my time there.

My time in senior football has had many ups and downs. Losing out in the playoffs twice and having to pick myself up and go again for pre-season training, knowing we were so close to the Football League with York City.

My proudest and greatest memory/achievement in football would be our Wembley double win in 2011/12. I was so fortunate to win at Wembley twice in eight days. It was the best week of my sporting career and something that I will never forget. I can remember walking up the famous steps of Wembley to collect the trophy like it was yesterday.

It was all the more sweet as I'd experienced heartache there twice previously. Once as captain, which was really tough to take. I had imagined leading my team to collect our winners' medals; a few years later it was worth the wait.

To play in front of 40,000 fans at Wembley is something I'd dreamed of and memories that I'll never forget. To work so hard in achieving something and then for all that hard work to have paid off. Sharing it with some good friends and having my family there with me in the stands. You can't get better than that."

Dan Parslow - York City FC

"My best experience as a player was at Wembley with Torquay getting promoted. I have been lucky enough to play there twice (and that could end up being more than a lot of Premier League players) but winning there is an unreal feeling.

Scoring for Notts County in front of fifteen-and-a-half thousand, to keep us in League One, on the last day of the season, was also an amazing feeling for different reasons. The club had been playing a 'Great Escape' theme for weeks as we looked doomed but staying up was as big as promotion at the time.

Scoring a 90th minute 30 yarder at home for Torquay United against Barnet was also incredible and was a catalyst for our play-off season and me getting in the League Two 'team of the year' in 2012.

These are things that I will never forget along with the day-to-day banter of being part of a team and all that goes with it."

Kevin Nicholson - Torquay United FC

Being a footballer is fantastic. There are not too many jobs where you can walk into work, keep fit, be happy and carry out work that you've loved, enjoyed and had an active obsession (and passion) for since childhood. So obviously there is a lot to love about the game and being part of it.

"When I was young, every day when I woke up, I just wanted to go outside and play football.

The best thing about being a professional footballer is waking up and playing football every day, especially when you have a good group of teammates and a manager that wants players to enjoy themselves.

I think, for any job, if you can wake up in the morning and look forward to going to work, no matter what that job is - you'll he happy and that's the most important thing for me. Waking up wanting to go to work and being happy!"

Jonte Smith - Crawley Town FC

"I've been fortunate enough to be at one of the biggest clubs in the world during its most successful period to date, under one of the best ever managers.

I first told my dad I wanted to play for Man United when I was six, so to actually do it is obviously very satisfying."

Ben Amos - Manchester United FC

"The best things about being a footballer are the fact you get to work outside, keeping yourself fit while playing a game you happily did for free as a kid, but now you get paid for it.

Not many people have hundreds/thousands of others singing their name as you go to work and when you are winning games and challenging at the top of your league (whatever level that may be) there is nothing better. Every day you carry that buzz and confidence around with you.

The thrill of competitive sport is also a huge positive. I've never met a footballer that isn't desperate to win whether it's a league game or a friendly game of snooker. Playing to win is like a drug and, win or lose, you want to go and do it all over again as soon as possible.

We are privileged to do what we do for a living and it's a job that a huge percentage of other people would do anything for."

Kevin Nicholson - Torquay United FC

"The best thing about being a pro is the whole atmosphere in the dressing room every day. Some days it can all be the same banter and same gags but it's still one of the best atmospheres you'll experience. That feeling of winning on a Saturday with your teammates and then enjoying that win the following week is fantastic!

I love playing football and wouldn't change it for anything. So many people want to become a footballer and we have to appreciate what we do and work hard to keep doing it.

Football banter will not be found anywhere else. If you were to take football banter into another workplace they wouldn't have a clue. You can't beat some of the stuff that goes on in the dressing room. People would think it's too vile, too rude, and too explicit, but in the football environment anything goes."

Matt Fish - Gillingham FC

"I just love everything the game has to offer really. It's something, as a child, I'd always wanted to do. And to be paid for doing something you love is an added bonus.

It's nice to have adulation from people and to make people smile on a Saturday afternoon when you have played well for their team.

At the end of the day the fans are who you play for really. If you can send fans home happy, after winning three points on a Saturday afternoon, I don't think there is any better feeling and it brings you huge satisfaction."

Mike Pollitt - Wigan FC

"*I love competition! And football is a great way of testing yourself. I think one of the things that makes football so appealing around the world, and the reason it's my favourite sport, is because you can play anywhere and with however many people. All you need is a football.*

I love that it has so many elements that really test you physically and mentally.

Being lucky enough to play football professionally is something I am very grateful for.

To be able to go into work each day, and go outside and play football, is something I could only have dreamt of growing up. I like the routine of being a professional; training throughout the week and then testing yourself in a game at the weekend. Then you try and do better and improve the next week. Being able to just focus on improving my game and getting better each day is something I love."

Chris Smalling - Manchester United FC

"*I am extremely fortunate that I get paid to do something that I love. From a very early age I imagined that I'd be a footballer and every morning I wake up and know I am extremely lucky.*

Like I've said before, I am not ashamed or embarrassed to admit that I've had to work very hard to get where I am today, playing in the Football League, and I never take it for granted.

I love training every day, keeping fit, being around some really good friends and then competing against somebody else when it comes to Saturday. I've always had a competitive side and sport is a great way of showing that."

Dan Parslow - York City FC

"I get to play a game that I have grown up and loved since being a young lad. I get to play every day in training, and play in front of thousands of fans with people who have the same ambitions and drive as myself.

The excitement I have every day of going to play football with the boys and kicking the ball around, whilst being paid, is great.

It's been my dream since I was a lad and I've got to a point now where I am playing in a very good league and I'm one step away from achieving my ultimate dream which is to play in the Premiership."

Craig Mackail-Smith - Brighton & Hove Albion FC

"A huge part of what I loved about being a footballer was the togetherness of the players, being part of something, the banter, the passion of the fans and - in the main - being around people you could rely on.

There are also parts of the game I dislike. For example, I don't like the way we are so quick to judge nowadays. Players are either very good or very bad; there are no in-betweens even though, in most cases, these players have the club at heart. The problem is that there are many people involved in football, making big decisions, who aren't exactly over-qualified to do so. This is why we see so many things in football happening that are, at times, hard to understand.

That said, I love the passion we have over here. I loved being part of a dressing room. I liked playing with good players, I found it more enjoyable."

Steve Claridge - Former Leicester, Portsmouth, Birmingham & Others

"I should mention that what I love particularly about football is that the players I have shared these moments with are now lifelong friends. We always have that common bond of having shared these experiences together. You almost become like a band of brothers and no matter how many weeks, months, or years you go without seeing them - when you do meet up, you carry on where you left off.

There is no question that football has given me the opportunity to meet people and make friends that wouldn't have been possible in any other job."

Neill Collins - Sheffield United FC

"Nothing beats getting paid for doing something you love. The feeling of coming out the tunnel to compete in front of thousands of fans is amazing.

I would go as far as saying being a professional footballer is the best job in the world."

Matt Parsons - Plymouth Argyle FC

"There are hundreds of things I love about being a professional footballer but when asked the question it is very difficult to give a specific answer.

Although it is a cliché, I love that I'm doing something as a job that I have enjoyed doing since I was a kid. I love the banter in the dressing room with the lads; I also enjoy the pressures that come with being a footballer.

I think if I was asked this question once I've finished playing there would be many answers which, at the moment, I take for granted. But 3 o'clock on a Saturday is the best thing about being a professional."

Peter Vincenti - Rochdale AFC

> *"I love the day-to-day involvement of being a footballer, having it on your passport, people asking you about it, and the constant interaction you have with people who want to be footballers and who want to be involved with football.*
>
> *I like the keeping fit aspect, also. I like playing in a game that I have always seen as enjoyable and in a game that I would have played for free. If you are given the opportunity to play and people are willing to pay for it, and outbid each other to capture your services for their club, it becomes an insane place sometimes.*
>
> *If someone had said to me: you can play but you won't get paid, I would have definitely still continued playing the game I love."*

Guy Branston (co-author) - a personal reflection

Becoming a footballer makes all the hard work, setbacks, and sacrifice worthwhile. Making a career in the game does require huge amounts of hard work, but the rewards and enjoyment you have will easily make it all worth it.

> *"Granted that the great experiences I've had were a drop in the ocean compared to the days of hard graft on the training pitch, but they were worth it 10 times over.*
>
> *There were times when I didn't think I would get there - I still haven't got where I want to be - but that was part of my journey and it kept me hungry. It was my love for football that got me through any tough times I had and the days when I genuinely wondered whether it was what I wanted.*
>
> *It's only natural to have tough days but it's the people who can drag themselves through them who will be successful. If you enjoy what you do then it's much easier to overcome tough times, and I for one would take training in the freezing cold over being stuck in an office any day! People pay money to play football and stay fit, we get paid to do it!!"*

Ben Amos - Manchester United FC

> *"Days like yesterday, playing in front of 30,000 people at Bramall Lane, and winning to go through to an FA Cup semi-final at Wembley, are definitely the moments that you most enjoy and remember.*
>
> *I have been very fortunate to enjoy three promotions with Wolves, Sunderland and Leeds and these moments are fantastic occasions. They certainly make all the hard work and sacrifices worthwhile."*
>
> **Neill Collins - Sheffield United FC**

Summary

Being part of football is great. If you can make it to the top and become a professional footballer then it's a chance to have a career you will love and enjoy.

Go for it with everything you've got and give yourself the best possible chance of achieving the dream you've had from a very young age. If you really want it, go and get it!

If you don't play at a professional level, and fall short, there is nothing stopping you from gaining a great deal of enjoyment from playing at an amateur level and working in an alternative industry and job role that you enjoy during the week.

The FA's funding and involvement in grassroots football means there is access to organized leagues across the country, giving you many opportunities to play in a local organized team in a competitive league, where points are at stake and trophies can be won.

Winning a match is a great feeling, and winning trophies and promotions is even better.

Sharing victories with thousands of adoring fans is unbelievable but, even if you play at an amateur level, rest assured that there are many highs and fun moments to be enjoyed with non-professional football as well.

The most important thing is enjoying your football and playing regularly. Whether that's in the Premier League or on a Sunday afternoon putting your own nets up before kick-off – football is a great sport to be involved in.

We wish you all the best on your road to becoming a professional footballer. Hard work, coupled with ability, desire and using the advice and guidance given throughout this book will put you in good stead to prosper - whatever position you find yourself in.

We are going to put more advice from readers and players onto our website. Do you have any advice you'd like to share? Want to learn more?

Visit **www.BennionKearny.com/share**

Contributors

Name: Ben Amos
Date of Birth: 10th April 1990
Nationality: English
Position: Goalkeeper
Plays for: Manchester United FC
Division: Premier League

My advice to football hopefuls…

Go at it fully committed. I've seen a lot of talented lads even before YTS level, with really good talent but they don't want to work.

They think it's their God-given right to become a professional footballer; their parents have told them since they were young: "you're going to be the next big thing."

They've not bothered at school and they've put all their eggs in one basket. If they had really thrown themselves at it, you'd say: "right, fair enough, that's what they want to do and that's their drive". But a lot of lads don't and just think they are destined to play in the Premier League. It's one thing having confidence in yourself and another leaving it down to chance and luck.

Name: Jack Baldwin
Date of Birth: 30th June 1993
Nationality: English
Position: Defender (Centre Back)
Plays for: Peterborough United FC
Division: Football League One

My advice to football hopefuls…

Follow your dream. If you want something bad enough, you will do everything you can to get it. However, at the same time I will say that until you are an established, experienced top flight footballer - the lifestyle of lots of money and fast cars is a far cry away. Don't get me wrong, getting paid to play football every day as your job, is amazing. You don't have the horrible hours of everyday office jobs, and you are always developing and learning something new. It is very hard work to get into, and once you are a pro it is even harder work to stay in the profession.

Good Luck! Enjoy the work. Work Hard, Play Hard.

Name: Steve Claridge
Date of Birth: 10th April 1966
Nationality: English
Position: Striker
Played for: Leicester, Portsmouth, Birmingham & Others
Division: Played in all professional divisions

My advice to football hopefuls...

Be as fit as you possibly can be. Be as strong as you can be. Be as prepared as you can be. And always, always give everything.

If you give everything: a) you'll have no regrets and b) nobody will get on your back; they will forgive you the mistakes and the odd bad game you have.

Someone said to me when I was growing up, "Never underestimate the power of effort over ability." That's something I took on-board and something I feel is a massive part of what you do.

There is not a player in the world who can say he is going to play well every game. However, what you *can* do is run around a lot and work hard. Obviously, you've got to be given the opportunity, and have a manager that knows what he wants and knows how to set the team up for you to do that. If, however, the manager doesn't do his job properly - players are often accused of lacking passion. That, in the main, isn't the case. It's because they don't believe in what they are doing.

Name: Neill Collins
Date of Birth: 2nd September 1983
Nationality: Scottish
Position: Defender (Centre Back)
Plays for: Sheffield United FC
Division: Football League One

My advice to football hopefuls…

The biggest thing for me is attitude. Having a 'good attitude' is sometimes easier said than done because football can be a cruel game, and people can really knock the stuffing out of you. I gave myself the best possible chance to be a professional footballer, I made sacrifices. I don't think some of the boys in the academies now make the sacrifices that even the first team players – guys who have played 300 games - are still making. The boys that can't get in the team don't realize why, and it's because they're not making the same sacrifices as those playing every week.

I would also advise you to have belief in yourself. I think you have to take it upon yourself to aid your progress and development. Too many people expect the coach to always tell them what to do, instead of just going out and doing extra running, doing extra weights, and doing extra football themselves. It's easy to say that when you've got experience behind you, but you need to be lucky enough to have someone in your family or a good coach tell you that.

Name: Matt Fish
Date of Birth: 5th January 1989
Nationality: English
Position: Defender (Right Back)
Plays for: Gillingham FC
Division: Football League One

My advice to football hopefuls…

Be prepared!

Football is so unpredictable; one day you may be the manager's favourite player, the next you could get injured or fall out of favour.

It is a good life but unless you're playing in the Championship (Top 10 clubs) or the Premiership it is a false life because, at the end of it, you're always going to have to get another job. You won't earn enough money to do nothing once you finish playing - unless you're at the top.

Enjoy it while you can but be prepared to go and try something new and eventually do something other than football. Be prepared to work hard and be pushed physically and mentally to the limit.

Name: Craig Mackail-Smith
Date of Birth: 25th February 1984
Nationality: Scottish
Position: Striker
Played for: Brighton & Hove Albion FC
Division: Championship

My advice to football hopefuls...

It's a balance. Have something outside football if it doesn't work out, and at the same time focus on improving yourself as a player, working hard, and taking the advice of everyone.

It could be helpful to write a program or make up some kind of schedule so that you train a bit, and then you study a bit. It is good if you have a plan in place and a way of organizing your time.

I think it would have helped me if I had written out more of a schedule, as it would have given me a better balance.

Also work rate is a big factor. Obviously you want to be technically gifted and great on the ball but sometimes you don't have those attributes. The one thing you can always have is work rate and the willingness to work hard. That will always bring you results.

Name: Jonathan Meades
Date of Birth: 2nd March 1992
Nationality: Welsh
Position: Defender (Left Back)
Plays for: Oxford United FC
Division: Football League Two

My advice to football hopefuls…

I would say 'train as you would play'. A lot of people, especially when you're younger, won't use training as preparation.

I've seen people with a lot of ability but they don't really try very hard in training. When it comes to matches they are not playing to their full potential.

Name: Kevin Nicholson
Date of Birth: 2nd October 1980
Nationality: English
Position: Defender (Left Back)
Plays for: Torquay United FC
Division: Football League Two

My advice to football hopefuls…

I would tell any young aspiring player to go for it completely with everything you've got.

Never give up and be totally committed as the rewards are amazing and the lifestyle second to none.

If all that fails; then move on and understand that football isn't the 'be all and end all' but know that you've given it every chance.

I hope to play at this level for a few more years but if I finish tomorrow I know I did everything physically possible to be the best I could be. I'd hoped for Premier League and I came up short but it wasn't for lack of trying. I've never drunk or done drugs, I've never gone out the night before games and I'd say the same to any young player. There's plenty of time to do all that stuff later, but you only have a very limited time being a professional player.

Name: Dan Parslow
Date of Birth: 11th September 1985
Nationality: Welsh
Position: Defender (Versatile)
Plays for: York City FC
Division: Football League Two

My advice to football hopefuls...

I know it's the old cliché but work as hard as you possibly can.

If you're fortunate to be given the opportunity in an academy there will be hundreds, possibly thousands of children who want that opportunity, so don't waste it.

Every time you turn up for training - give your best. If your best isn't good enough, you can hold your hands up, look yourself in the mirror, and accept you couldn't have done any more.

That's how I've got where I am today, just through hard work. There have been players that were probably more gifted than me with the football but they maybe haven't quite got the drive or character to get where they wanted to be.

Name: Matt Parsons
Date of Birth: 25th December 1991
Nationality: English
Position: Defender (Left Back)
Plays for: Plymouth Argyle
Division: Football League Two

My advice to football hopefuls...

Never give up on your dream, no matter how hard times get! I've always liked the saying and told myself it time and time again, "Tough times don't last, but tough people do".

You shouldn't put all your eggs into one basket. You should always concentrate in school to get the best possible grades. Education will help you outside football if things don't work out.

Name: Matt Piper
Date of Birth: 29th September 1981
Nationality: English
Position: Midfield (Winger)
Played for: Leicester City FC & Sunderland AFC
Division: Premier League

My advice to football hopefuls...

Without a doubt make sure you try and do well at school. Get some qualifications and have a plan, a set goal, and find interests other than football. Still concentrate 100% on football but find something else that you enjoy doing, maybe not as much as football, but something you can do after football.

Whether it finishes through injury like me, or you have a full career, even if you've earned enough money to never work again you'll still want to do something.

Try and think about what that next thing will be after football and put measures in place to have that thing ready when you finish, because it will end one day.

When I look back, so many people told me so: older pros, coaches, physiotherapists I worked with when I was injured. But, no matter who said it to me, all I wanted was to be a footballer and I didn't listen. But now, with hindsight, I realise just how important that advice was.

Name: Mike Pollitt
Date of Birth: 29th February 1972
Nationality: English
Position: Goalkeeper
Plays for: Wigan Athletic FC
Division: Championship

My advice to football hopefuls…

It's the same old thing, make sure you work hard. I've always said you never get anything for nothing and I feel it's a major ingredient for any young player that wants to become a top player. It's all about hard work and practicing.

If you look at the top players they practice all the time. It's the same in any other sport: you won't get to where you want to be without working hard.

There are obviously other things you can talk about but for me working hard is the main ingredient for any young player aspiring to be a professional footballer. I preach that to the young lads.

A lot of the lads do their training and go straight home and play on the XBOX in the afternoon, but you are never going to get any better doing that.

Sometimes you have to put the extra miles in, and do that extra shift, to get that additional 1% out of your body!

Name: Chris Smalling
Date of Birth: 22nd November 1989
Nationality: English
Position: Defender (Centre Back)
Plays for: Manchester United FC
Division: Premier League

My advice to football hopefuls…

My main piece of advice that I'd stress to young kids is to enjoy playing football. Without that you will never achieve happiness and in doing so never maximize your own potential. Whether it is playing in the garden with your friends, or on a Sunday afternoon with your local team, never stop smiling.

Name: Jonte Smith
Date of Birth: 10th July 1994
Nationality: Bermudian
Position: Striker
Plays for: Crawley Town FC
Division: Football League One

My advice to football hopefuls...

Don't be discouraged; if you're determined enough and work hard enough you can make it.

Name: Chris Stokes
Date of Birth: 8th March 1991
Nationality: English
Position: Defender (Left Back)
Plays for: Forest Green Rovers FC
Division: Conference Premier

My advice to football hopefuls...

I advise all young players to work hard at school, as you never know what can happen in the future.

I also advise young people who want to be footballers to never give up on the dream. Football is full of setbacks, so stay strong and put the maximum effort into every game you play as you don't know if that game could be your last.

Sacrifice nights out and drinking alcohol - there is plenty of time to enjoy yourself when you retire. You only get out of football what you put into it.

Name: Peter Vincenti
Date of Birth: 7th July 1986
Nationality: Jersey
Position: Midfielder (Winger)
Plays for: Rochdale AFC
Division: Football League Two

My advice to football hopefuls…

I would say first and foremost you have to enjoy it, because if you enjoy your football then it becomes a lot easier. The reason you choose to pursue football as a kid is because you enjoy it so why shouldn't you continue to do so? You have to try and keep that enjoyment going.

Never let your highs be too high or your lows be too low. I think that's important.

Obviously when you develop as a footballer and move into your career there are different pressures you have to deal with, but at the end of the day you need to enjoy the pressure and try to embrace it.

Graduation: Life Lessons of a Professional Footballer by Richard Lee

The 2010/11 season will go down as a memorable one for Goalkeeper Richard Lee. Cup wins, penalty saves, hypnotherapy and injury would follow, but these things only tell a small part of the tale. Filled with anecdotes, insights, humour and honesty - Graduation uncovers Richard's campaign to take back the number one spot, save a lot of penalties, and overcome new challenges. What we see is a transformation - beautifully encapsulated in this extraordinary season.

"Whatever level you have played the beautiful game and whether a goalkeeper or outfield player, you will connect with this book. Richard's honesty exposes the fragility in us all, he gives an honest insight into dimensions of a footballer's life that are often kept a secret and in doing so offers worthy advice on how to overcome any hurdle. A great read." **Ben Foster, Goalkeeper, West Bromwich Albion.**

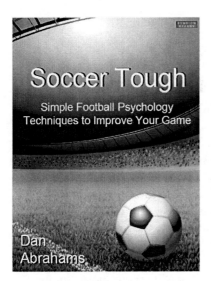

Soccer Tough by Dan Abrahams

"Take a minute to slip into the mind of one of the world's greatest soccer players and imagine a stadium around you. Picture a performance under the lights and mentally play the perfect game."

Technique, speed and tactical execution are crucial components of winning soccer, but it is mental toughness that marks out the very best players – the ability to play when pressure is highest, the opposition is strongest, and fear is greatest. Top players and coaches understand the importance of sport psychology in soccer but how do you actually train your mind to become the best player you can be?

Soccer Tough demystifies this crucial side of the game and offers practical techniques that will enable soccer players of all abilities to actively develop focus, energy, and confidence. Soccer Tough will help banish the fear, mistakes, and mental limits that holds players back.

Scientific Approaches to Goalkeeping in Football: A practical perspective on the most unique position in sport
by Andy Elleray

Do you coach goalkeepers and want to help them realise their fullest potential? Are you a goalkeeper looking to reach the top of your game? Then search no further and dive into this dedicated goalkeeping resource. Written by goalkeeping guru Andy Elleray this book offers a fresh and innovative approach to goalkeeping in football. With a particular emphasis on the development of young goalkeepers, it sheds light on training, player development, match performances, and player analysis. Utilising his own experiences Andy shows the reader various approaches, systems and exercises that will enable goalkeepers to train effectively and appropriately to bring out the very best in them.

Small Time: A Life in the Football Wilderness by Justin Bryant

In 1988, 23-year-old American goalkeeper Justin Bryant thought a glorious career in professional football awaited him. He had just saved two penalties for his American club - the Orlando Lions - against Scotland's Dunfermline Athletic, to help claim the first piece of silverware in their history. He was young, strong, healthy, and confident.

Small Time is the story of a life spent mostly in the backwaters of the game. As Justin negotiated the Non-League pitches of the Vauxhall-Opel League, and the many failed professional leagues of the U.S. in the 1980s and 90s - Football, he learned, is 95% blood, sweat, and tears; but if you love it enough, the other 5% makes up for it.

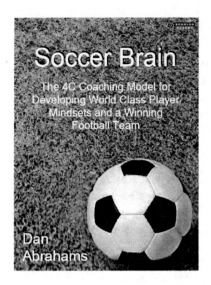

Soccer Brain: The 4C Coaching Model for Developing World Class Player Mindsets and a Winning Football Team
by Dan Abrahams

Coaching soccer is demanding. Impossible to perfect, it requires a broad knowledge of many performance areas including technique, tactics, psychology and the social aspects of human development. The first two components are covered in detail in many texts – but Soccer Brain uniquely offers a comprehensive guide to developing the latter two – player mindsets and winning teams.

Soccer Brain is for the no limits coach. It's for the coach who is passionate about developing players and building a winning team. This is not a traditional soccer coaching book filled with drills or tactics or playing patterns. This book is about getting the very best from you, the coach, and helping you develop a coaching culture of excellence and world class football mindsets.

Saturday Afternoon Fever: A Year On The Road For Soccer Saturday
by Johnny Phillips

You might already know Johnny Phillips. He is a football reporter for Sky Sports' Soccer Saturday programme and a man who gets beamed into the homes of fans across the country every weekend.

For the 2012/13 season, Johnny decided to do something different. He wanted to look beneath the veneer of household-name superstars and back-page glamour to chronicle a different side to our national sport. As Johnny travelled the country, he found a game that he loved even more, where the unheralded stars were not only driven by a desire to succeed but also told stories of bravery and overcoming adversity, often to be plucked from obscurity into the spotlight… and sometimes dropped back into obscurity again. Football stories that rarely see the limelight but have a value all fans can readily identify with.

Jose Mourinho by Ciaran Kelly

From growing up in a Portugal emerging from dictatorship, and struggling to live up to his father's legacy as an international goalkeeper, the book details José Mourinho's extraordinary journey: the trophies, tragedies and, of course, the fall-outs. Starting out as a translator for the late Sir Bobby Robson, Mourinho has come to define a new breed of manager, with his unrivalled use of psychology, exhaustive research, and man management providing ample compensation for an unremarkable playing career. Mourinho has gone on to become one of the greatest managers of all-time.

From Porto to Chelsea, and Inter to Real Madrid – the Mourinho story is as intriguing as the man himself. Now, a new challenge awaits at Stamford Bridge. Covering the Mourinho story to October 2013 and featuring numerous exclusive interviews with figures not synonymous with the traditional Mourinho narrative.

Conference Season
by Steve Leach

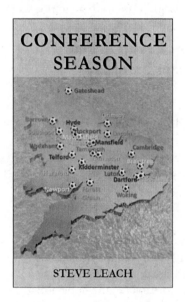

Disillusioned with the corporate ownership, mega-bucks culture, and overpaid prima donnas, of the Premiership, Steve Leach embarked on a journey to rediscover the soul of professional football. His journey, over the 2012/13 season, took him to twenty-four different Football Conference towns and fixtures, visiting venues as diverse as the Impact Arena in Alfreton, Stonebridge Road in Ebbsfleet, and Luton's Kenilworth Road.

Encountering dancing bears at Nuneaton, demented screamers at Barrow, and 'badger pasties' at rural Forest Green – Steve unearthed the stories behind the places and people – it was a journey that showed just how football and communities intertwine, and mean something.

Conference Season is a warm and discerning celebration of the diversity of towns and clubs which feature in the Conference, and of the supporters who turn up week-after-week to cheer their teams on.